St. Louis Community College

Forest Park
Florissant Valley
Meramec

Instructional Resources
St. Louis, Missouri

What's Really Said
in the
Teachers' Lounge

CORWIN
PRESS

The Corwin Press logo—a raven striding across an open book—represents the happy union of courage and learning. We are a professional-level publisher of books and journals for K-12 educators, and we are committed to creating and providing resources that embody these qualities. Corwin's motto is "Success for All Learners."

What's Really Said

in the

Teachers' Lounge

*Provocative Ideas About
Cultures and Classrooms*

Jeffrey A. Kottler

CORWIN PRESS, INC.
A Sage Publications Company
Thousand Oaks, California

For information:

Corwin Press, Inc.
A Sage Publications Company
2455 Teller Road
Thousand Oaks, California 91320
E-mail: order@corwin.sagepub.com

SAGE Publications Ltd.
6 Bonhill Street
London EC2A 4PU
United Kingdom

SAGE Publications India Pvt. Ltd.
M-32 Market
Greater Kailash I
New Delhi 110 048 India

Printed in the United States of America

Library of Congress Cataloging-in-Publication Data

Kottler, Jeffrey A.
    What's really said in the teacher's lounge : provocative ideas
about cultures and classrooms / author, Jeffrey A. Kottler.
       p.   cm.
    Includes bibliographical references and index.
    ISBN 0-8039-6337-8 (cloth). — ISBN 0-8039-6338-6 (pbk.)
       1. Educational anthropology—United States. 2. Multicultural
education—United States. 3. Teachers—United States—Social
conditions. 4. Classroom environment—United States. I. Title.
LB45.K68   1997
306.43—dc21   96-51211

This book is printed on acid-free paper.

97 98 99 00 01 02 03 10 9 8 7 6 5 4 3 2 1

Production Editor: Sherrise M. Purdum
Production Assistant: Denise Santoyo
Editorial Assistant: Janet Westenberg
Typesetter/Designer: Christina M. Hill
Cover Designer: Marcia R. Finlayson

Contents

Preface   ix
   Acknowledgments   xi

About the Author and Contributors   xiii

PART I: CONCEPTUAL PROVOCATIONS

1. Your Culture Is Showing   3

   What Is Culture?   6
   Cultural Adaptability   7
   Giving Lip Service to What Is Politically Correct   8
   Revealing Yourself   9
   Origins of Cultural Identity   12
   Cultural Values   14
   Culture as Individuality   18

2. Climate of Political Correctness   19

   One Slip and You Are Under Arrest!   20
   That the Poor and Weak Shall Wither 23

Tribal Wars   25
Politics of Victimization   28
Some Questionable Assumptions   30
More Alike Than Different   34
Scapegoats   36
Reversing 100,000 Years of History   37

3. Just How Different Are We, Anyway?   41

Disorientation Facing Different Cultures   43
Entrenched Positions and Changing Cultural Values   44
Cultures of Teachers, Students, and Schools   48
Teacher Subcultures   53
Multiple Cultures That Interact   55
Confronting Biases and Prejudices   56

4. Some Cultural Misunderstandings   60

It Always Worked Before   60
Neglect or Overreaction?   63
Your Role in the Conflict   66
A Clash of Cultures   70

5. Beauty and Grace in School Rituals   75

Richard Powell and *Jeffrey A. Kottler*

Structure of Rituals   77
Then and Now   78
Industrialization of School Rituals   80
Becoming Ritualized   83
Toward a New Social Imagination for Schooling   86
Accommodating Student Rituals   88

BRIDGE

6. Teaching as if You Were an Anthropologist   93

The Culture of an Anthropologist   93
Alternative Teacher Roles   95
What It Means to Be an Anthropologist   96

Traveling Like an Anthropologist   104
Get Out and Walk   111
Cultural Lessons for the Teacher   113
Within the Borders of Your Community   115

PART II: PURPOSEFUL ACTIONS

7. Being and Doing Things Differently in the Classroom   119

   Jeffrey A. Kottler and *Ellen Kottler*

   Being Rather Than Doing   120
   Work Within the Student's Culture   123
   Learning the Rules Within Student Cultures   124
   Making Learning Culturally Relevant   126
   Some Things You Can Do   127

8. Narrative Approaches to Culture and Learning   133

   Gerald Monk and *Jeffrey A. Kottler*

   Narrative Approach   136
   Brief Review of Constructivist Theory   137
   Differences in Adult and Child Knowledge   138
   Application of Narrative Approaches in the Classroom   139
   Jeremy's Story   143
   The Dominant Story   144
   Using Externalizations in Narrative Questioning   145
   Relative Influence Questions   147
   Assembling the Alternative Story   150
   Narrative Teaching and Cultural Sensitivity   151

9. Internationalizing the Classroom   153

   Elaine Jarchow and *Jeffrey A. Kottler*

   Why Internationalize the Classroom?   153
   When Teachers Model an International Perspective   155
   Making Learning Last   159
   Activities for the Elementary School Classroom   160
   Activities for the Junior or Senior High School   162
   Additional Resources   166

10. What Matters Most   169

    Not Feeling Welcome   170
    Those Who Are Misunderstood   171
    When Teachers Have Trouble   173
    So, What Matters Most?   175

References   179

Preface

What's Really Said in the Teachers' Lounge is written as much for the heart as for the head. There has certainly been much attention directed toward cultural diversity in education in the past decade, much of it thought provoking and stimulating, especially with regard to changes in how we operate in our schools. Many of our efforts have been largely superficial, however, giving lip service to what is politically correct rather than addressing the deeper issues that lie at the foundation of our difficulties in the classroom and in misunderstandings with children who are unresponsive to our best efforts.

This book is not for everyone. As the title implies, I believe there is considerable hypocrisy, if not dishonesty, in how many of us publicly espouse certain values related to honoring cultural diversity when, in fact, we only go through the motions of doing what appears to be professionally appropriate. I am certainly as guilty as most. Although I teach courses in multicultural counseling and education, work with diverse student populations throughout North America and the Pacific Rim, and proclaim myself to be among the enlightened, when I get together with trusted friends and colleagues my own biases and prejudices slip out. I sit around and complain about how unappreciated I feel, how students are not what they used to be, and how it is mostly their fault for being so lazy, unmotivated, and resistant to all the good stuff I have to offer. Once I leave the safety of the teachers' lounge, I put on my best face as the most caring, compassionate, flexible, and culturally sensitive instructor around. Sometimes, I even manage to act that way.

I have tried to make this an honest, intimate, provocative, and haunting book that emphasizes process as much as content and that speaks to your innermost core—your own cultural background that led you to the role of teacher and that both guides and limits you in your work with others. I expect that many of the ideas presented will stir things up a bit. The point is that we are so careful not to offend anyone that honest opinions are often limited to the teachers' lounge. Multiculturalism has become so politically correct that authentic feelings and honest opinions have gone underground. What is described as sensitivity to diversity is often transformed into a degree of caution in which people no longer say what they really think, except in the company of a few trusted friends. Furthermore, there is a backlash of resentment festering among many teachers who feel they have lost their freedom to express what they really feel.

Racism and oppression have diminished a little, maybe even a lot, in the past few decades—but not nearly enough. One reason for the discrepancies between appearances and reality is that teachers are expected only to make token gestures of compliance to multicultural values rather than dramatic transformations in how they work.

This is a book for those who are willing to look in the mirror; I urge you not to argue with me but rather with yourself.

What's Really Said in the Teachers' Lounge is intended to help teachers at all phases of professional development explore how their own cultural origins, as well as those of their students and colleagues, impact growth and learning. Far more than a "how-to" collection of classroom techniques, the intent is to help educators develop greater cultural sensitivity and integrate ideas into a model that is more responsive to the needs of diverse children. Equally significant is practicing greater congruence between what we say is so important and what we actually do in our professional and personal lives.

The book is organized into two parts, with a bridge between them. Part I explores issues related to culture, especially those that are provocative and that have been ignored in many public forums. My intent is to challenge you, the reader, to really examine some of your most deeply held convictions surrounding your culture as well as those of people around you.

The bridge chapter connects the theory in Part I to the action in Part II. By thinking in alternative ways about your role as a teacher, it is possible to do some things very differently in your work and life. This includes not only creative and flexible methods of instruction, discipline, and motivation but also ways to make your classroom more vibrant and culturally responsive.

Acknowledgments

I am most indebted to Richard Powell of Texas Tech University for his help in conceptualizing the book and for his contribution as coauthor of Chapter 5. I also thank Elaine Jarchow of Texas Tech University, Gerald Monk of the University of Waikato in New Zealand, and Ellen Kottler of Western High School in Las Vegas for their work as coauthors of chapters in this book. I am indebted to George Spindler of Stanford University, Louis Mirón of the University of California at Irvine, Christine Finnan of the Center of Excellence in Accelerating Learning, and Harvey Alvy of Eastern Washington University for their thoughtful, critical, and constructive reviews of a previous version of the manuscript. Finally, it was Gracia Alkema, the visionary behind Corwin Press, who encouraged me to find the courage and honesty to explore some aspects of myself, and the field of education, that are very painful to examine.

Jeffrey A. Kottler
Las Vegas
March, 1997

About the
Author and Contributors

Jeffrey A. Kottler is Professor of Education at Texas Tech University in Lubbock, Texas. He is author or coauthor of 25 books in the fields of psychology and education, including *On Being a Teacher* (1993), *Teacher as Counselor* (1993), *Beyond Blame: A New Way of Resolving Conflicts in Relationships* (1994), *Classrooms Under the Influence: Addicted Families, Addicted Students* (1995), *Growing a Therapist* (1995), and *The Language of Tears* (1996).

Elaine Jarchow is Dean of the College of Education at Texas Tech University. In her contributions to Chapter 9 on globalizing the classroom, she demonstrates her expertise as a world traveler, having consulted with teachers throughout the Pacific Rim, Southeast Asia, and Eastern Europe. She is coeditor of *Preparing Teachers to Teach Global Perspectives: A Handbook for Teacher Educators*, published by Corwin Press.

Ellen Kottler is Social Studies Curriculum Specialist for Clark County Schools, Nevada. She has written two other books, both published by Corwin Press: *Teacher as Counselor: Developing the Help-*

ing Skills You Need and *Children With Limited English: Teaching Strategies for the Regular Classroom.*

Gerald Monk is Senior Lecturer at the University of Waikato in Hamilton, New Zealand, where he directs programs in narrative counseling and teaching. He is a coeditor of *Narrative Therapy in Practice: The Archaeology of Hope.*

Richard Powell is Associate Professor of Education at Texas Tech University. He is coauthor of *Classrooms Under the Influence: Addicted Families, Addicted Students* and *Field Experience: Strategies for Exploring Diversity in Schools.*

Part I

Conceptual Provocations

Your Culture Is Showing

Who are you?

However you would answer that question—as a teacher, a wife, a Christian, an Italian American, a woman, a father, or any of a dozen other role identities—signals the most predominant features of your cultural affiliations. Each one of us is made up of the sum total of our cultural identities. We are not a single self but rather a collection of selves, each one influenced by what we have lived before, what we are living now, and how we hope to live in the future.

So many cultures make up a part of who you are—for example, the culture of your gender, political affiliations, socioeconomic class, marital status, sexual orientation, ethnic background, religious identification, and even your chronological age. Furthermore, each of these cultures interacts with one another and with the cultures that are part of each person you meet.

For example, a new student enters your classroom, shyly holding out a crumpled piece of paper that appears to be an official school form. Before you reach for the pink slip, you take a moment to study this new person who will share space with you for the next year. Lost in your momentary contemplation, you are startled by the realization that he is studying you just as carefully as you are checking him out. If we could enter both your minds at that moment, we would hear a barrage of internal questions:

Teacher: Well, he looks cooperative enough, but of course, appearances can be deceiving.

Student: Look at her. Giving me the once-over. As if I am some piece of meat she is dying to cut into.

Teacher: What's with that big comb sticking out of his pocket? Could that really be just for grooming? It looks more like a weapon. And he doesn't have enough hair for a comb that big.

Student: I can't believe it! This lady's wearing shoes my grandmother wouldn't even be caught in.

Teacher: This little guy could be trouble. Gonna have to watch him carefully. I think I'll put him in front, just so I can keep an eye on him.

Student: She's going to be mean. I can tell already. I bet she puts me in front so she can watch me every minute.

So goes the kind of internal dialogue in which any two people, including a teacher and student meeting for the first time, try to size up one another. These first impressions, however distorted and biased based on limited data, help us deal with new interpersonal situations by giving us a starting point for future interactions.

Much of the internal processing that is going on inside us during a first meeting with a new student (or any person) is based on preliminary judgments about where this person will fit into our scheme of things. Will this student be a help or a hindrance? Is this kid bright or will he or she need extra time and energy? What is going to work best to motivate this student and capture his or her interest? How can I handle this student if he or she gets out of line?

Although each of the previous questions leads to an answer that can be determined by the student's individual behavior over time, initially you construct hypotheses based on your prior experiences with others who remind you of this particular student. Just as the student is making some assumptions about you, based on your dress and various nonverbal cues, so too are you making some initial predictions about what this student may be like. Although it is hoped that both of you will alter your perceptions based more on how you really are as individuals rather than as projected images, much depends on the extent to which you are willing to give the other person the benefit of the doubt.

It is also fascinating to consider that no matter how much we attempt to hide or disguise our own cultural origins, other people make assumptions based on limited cues available. How we express ourselves—in vocabulary, syntax, grammar, intonation, and accent—reveals something about where we came from. Our manner of dress, the way we carry ourselves, and physical features related to our size, gender, skin color, hair texture, and facial features present others with data that they use to classify us according to cultures with which they have prior experience.

People are thus constantly thinking in terms of culture, trying to make some decisions related to values that matter most to them: Are you like me or different from me? Will you be on my side or against me? If you give me trouble, how might I protect myself most successfully? Although such prejudgments, based on such limited information, do lead to misperceptions, prejudices, and other mistakes, such cognitive activity is also quite useful in making predictions about future behavior, especially if perceptions are altered in light of new, updated information. Because part of the teacher's job is to accurately read exactly how to reach each individual student to promote growth and learning, cultural diagnostics are crucial to forming preliminary plans for how to initiate and respond in many situations. For example, before you discover that Melinda is oversensitive to criticism, that Mikail does not like to be asked to speak out loud, or that Esperanza will answer questions correctly if you prod her several times, you rely first on prior cultural experiences. You know, for example, that among the particular age group and community you are working with (a) boys volunteer more often than girls, (b) Catholic and Mormon children are more prone to approval seeking than the Lutherans, (c) children from the southeast part of the city who are more economically disadvantaged require more time to complete their homework assignments, (d) native Spanish speakers need special help with their spelling to include the silent letter "h," and (e) children from the wealthier neighborhoods require more structured limit setting because of a sense of entitlement. These, of course, are just a few ways that a teacher might establish a set of differential guidelines for students, depending on their cultural origins.

Although these are starting points, they also represent gross generalizations that will not apply to particular individuals.

What Is Culture?

When speaking about the culture of an individual, or how that
behavior is shaped and patterned by prior social experiences, it is
useful to define more clearly the parameters about which we are
speaking. Culture, for example, refers to far more than simply our
ethnicity, but if this term applies to everything in the past that
influences our present and future behavior then it also loses its
precision in focusing on particular types of prior experience.

Culture is broadly defined as socially transmitted patterns of
thought and behavior, including values, attitudes, characteristics,
and artifacts. These norms for our behavior are established by our
home environment and by what takes place in school, mostly at the
hands of peers but to some extent by teachers. Culture is neither an
influence nor a dimension but rather, according to Spindler and
Spindler (1993), a process that is part of everything that we think,
feel, say, or do. Furthermore, Spindler and Spindler make the crucial
point that is central to a theme in *What's Really Said in the Teachers'
Lounge:* Teachers who do not know their own culture cannot deal
effectively with those of others.

There are two kinds of culture that I speak of, the first of which
is what we normally associate as our primary cultural identity—that
is, those behaviors and attitudes that have been programmed by our
ethnic, religious, and national identities. This traditional view of
culture also includes what Gollnick and Chinn (1994) label "microcultures," or subsocieties, that have unique cultural patterns. A given
student or teacher, for example, may share some characteristics of the
female gender microculture but may also identify strongly with
values implicit in other microcultures that are dominant at various
times—feminism, urban upper-middle class, Greek American, recov-
ering alcoholics, or readers of science fiction.

There also resides within each of us, as human beings and as
teachers, a culture that is far more individualized. This identity is as
unique as our fingerprints, composed of what has been instilled in
us by our parents and extended family and legacies passed on from
our ancestors. This culture, however, has also been shaped by every

book we have ever read, every movie we have viewed, and every conversation we have had. It is not just the result of systematic efforts on the part of teachers, ministers, politicians, authors, behavioral scientists, and advertising and marketing executives to influence us to fit their molds (which certainly is their agenda); it is also the result of our own individual efforts and choices to create a culture within. This internal template is only part of what some educational psychologists think of as "self concept." It is far more than that, however, encompassing the sum total of all aspects of our past and present experience that influence what we like and what we avoid, where and how we feel most uncomfortable, and what we want and how we intend to get it.

Although I speak of "the" culture as if there is only one, each of us is made up of multiple cultures that are continuously in transition from one to another. In addition to the cultures of our family, our friends, our ethnicity and religion, and our gender and social class, there are also the particular cultures of our school. We are all continuously making border crossings from one world to another (Phelan, Davidson, & Yu, 1993). We speak one kind of language, think and react in a particular way, when we are with our students, another with our colleagues, and still another with friends or siblings or with parents or our children. The rules of interaction and the norms for what is acceptable and unacceptable behavior change significantly as we traverse one world and enter another.

Cultural Adaptability

In your role as teacher, you radiate confidence and authority. You stand before a room full of students utterly in control of yourself and the situation. A few hours later, however, you are in another classroom— this time as a student yourself—and you are tongue-tied, fearful of saying or doing the wrong thing, and concerned that others will find out you are incompetent or stupid. Once safely back in your own home, you take charge of things once again, feeling utterly secure in this culture you have cocreated with your family. Then the phone rings: It is your parents. Once again, you become deferential. You ricochet back and forth all day long from one culture to another depending on the circumstances, just as does each of your students. We are all continuously making cultural adaptions according to what is needed.

This ability to adapt from what Spindler and Spindler (1994) call the "enduring self" to various "situated selves" is the key for many children (and adults) to achieving success in different situations. This is, in fact, the function of culture that helps people accommodate to particular environmental conditions. For example, in Greenland, a culture has evolved that helps its inhabitants master the challenges related to ice and snow and seals and polar bears. The gang culture of the urban ghetto has similarly evolved as a means by which to help young people survive in the face of poverty, isolation, and ethnic territorial boundaries. Likewise, distinct cultures have developed in every classroom in every school as the norms by which both children and teachers can guide their own behavior and attempt to influence the actions of others.

How well we do our jobs as teachers depends, to a great extent, on our ability and willingness to help diverse students make necessary adjustments in their behavior from one peer or home culture to a classroom culture without compromising their essential prized values. Of course, this also presumes that we can make similar adaptions in our own thinking and behavior according to what is most appropriate.

Giving Lip Service to
What Is Politically Correct

What is teaching except the attempt to help someone acquire skills or knowledge he or she does not have and perceives to be valuable? To accomplish this task, it is presumed that we would have at our disposal certain crucial information: What is it the person we are teaching already knows and can do? Just as important: How does this person characteristically operate internally so that we can communicate in such a way that what we have to offer is likely to be heard, acknowledged, understood, and used constructively?

What's Really Said in the Teachers' Lounge is about aspects of the second question that are often ignored. Certainly, considerable efforts are extended in teacher training, and even continuing education, to understand the process of a child's cognitive functioning and information processing. There is also lip service paid to other variables that affect how a learner relates to the world, including language and culture.

In fact, there are few dimensions of education receiving more attention these days than the multicultural and pluralistic composition of our classrooms. Despite all the research being conducted on the impact of culture on learning and teaching, however, there is often a superficial treatment of the subject. It is as if we are all going through the motions of what is hot these days, what is politically correct and fashionable, by using the right terms and celebrating diversity—when it is convenient and profitable.

Much of the literature being generated and many of the training programs that are conducted come across with the same messages over and over again: You are not doing your job adequately because you are failing to recognize and attend to the cultural differences of the children you are working with. As such, you are reaching the children who mostly resemble you in basic values and culture. You should feel guilty about this neglect on your part—it is evidence of your latent or overt racism. Furthermore, you are scolded for being ethnocentric, marginalizing those who are different.

I do not quibble with these statements. In fact, I agree with them wholeheartedly. I simply wonder, however, if there is not much more to this cultural puzzle. If we examine the cultures within each of us, we find that individual identity is composed of a dominant culture or two, several microcultures that vie for influence depending on the situation, and a host of other social factors that emanate from our family and peer groups.

Revealing Yourself

What is it that someone would need to know about your cultural heritage to understand you? What have been the most significant influences on your own cultural development?

The reason you are a teacher in the first place (or training to be one) is related to your unique history growing up. Actually, it is fascinating to trace the series of events—some serendipitous and some the result of deliberate choices—that led you to your current career.

Go back to your very first memory of school—the very first hazy image you have of being in a classroom. Try to recall not just the visual memory of seeing yourself in a particular place but also the feelings that were most prevalent for you at that time.

I have two distinct memories, the first of which is fairly vague. I must have been in preschool and I was playing with blocks. They had splinters. I remember another child, a boy I think, who impressed me with his propensity for eating Scotch tape. The feeling I associate with this experience is mild curiosity, if not amusement.

The most distinct memory occurred in first grade. My teacher's name was Mrs. Silver and she was proud of her nickname, "Eagle Eye Silver," because she claimed she could see everything we were doing at every moment. Once, I remember testing this challenge. The teacher had her back to us, staring out the window, but more likely she was studying our reflection in the glass. Bored with our handwriting practice, I stuck a pencil in my nose and let it dangle. My "neighbor" thought this was pretty funny, so I stuck a pencil in the other nostril and pretended they were walrus tusks. Although my friend was amused mightily, Mrs. Silver assuredly was not: She made me stand in front of the whole class with pencils in my nose until my humiliation was total and complete.

Needless to say, my first memory of school was not a precious one. It did, however, have a major impact on future directions I would take. What about your own experiences?

From school, journey now to your home as a child in which you were involved in some ritual together with your family. This could have been a religious activity or, just as likely, some habit that was part of the unique way your family ate together or settled disputes.

While you are still in this mode of thought, bring to mind the recollection of the taste or smell of one special food that you associate with growing up in your home. Recall a dish, or even a collection of them, that best represented your identified culture.

What about language as well? Even if your parents and grandparents were third- or fourth-generation immigrants, you likely had some expressions, phrases, or words that were part of your ethnic heritage.

Think about what most distinguished you from other children—not just your individual characteristics but also the combination of cultural identities related to your religion, gender, family, and ethnicity.

When you combine all these remembrances of the past, what you have is an incomplete image of yourself as a cultural being—one who is the product of foods, customs, language, history, media, habits, values, and knowledge about your role in life.

It is no coincidence that you are a teacher. What kind of teacher you are, as well, resulted from not only your formal education but also your cultural upbringing.

Now you stand in front of a roomful of kids and you have personal reactions to every one of them. Some you like more than others. Some make your stomach churn. Some you would not mind taking home with you, and others you would turn away from if you saw them on the street. Some children you see as having great potential and others as likely losers. Some of them you will give extra effort and patience to, whereas others get your bare minimum attention.

You do not like this part of you. Surely, you would not admit your preferences outside of your trusted friends. The reality, however, is that some kids you like and others you do not like. Although you would defend your judgment with the claim that certain children have earned your disapproval, the truth of the matter is that perceptions are based on not only what people do but also how we interpret their actions.

You ask a child to do something and she defiantly says "No!" How you will respond at that moment depends on the following factors:

1. What the context of this behavior is
2. What you think the child is really saying to you: "I'm in a bad mood," "I will do it in a minute," or "Go to hell!"
3. How others are reacting to the public challenge
4. What your level of control is at that moment

If you are honest with yourself, you would also have to admit that you might react rather differently if this child was a large boy versus a little girl or if the child was a member of one cultural group versus another.

As much as we might guard against our biases, we all have preferences based on perceived similarity. I gravitate toward children who are most like me when I was a child. I do this unconsciously, even though I know to watch for this tendency. Inside my head, I can hear myself applauding the "class clown" all the while taking appropriate steps to censure inappropriate behavior. Similarly, when a passive, withdrawn child refuses to respond, I can feel my patience running thin.

None of us treat all children the same, regardless of our best intentions. Furthermore, I suggest that the origins for our preferences are found in our own cultural heritage.

Origins of Cultural Identity

Like most teachers, I am the result of a rich blend of cultures. My maternal grandparents emigrated from Sweden, and my father's parents emigrated from Russia during the time when Jews were systematically persecuted. Although I have white skin and blue eyes, fitting in quite nicely with the majority culture, there are many people who identify me as an oppressed minority. I do not practice my religion actively but clearly identify ethnically with my ancestral heritage. It would be fair to say that, like many Jews, I am waiting for the next inevitable wave of genocide that occurs every generation or so to wipe out my family. I have vowed that I will not go without a fight.

Being Jewish, however, is hardly the primary basis for my culture that shapes me as a human being and as a teacher. I was born to the upper-middle class, and although education and achievement were certainly values that were part of my upbringing, there were other forces that shaped me as well. I am a child of the 1960s and the product of a dysfunctional family that eventually resulted in my parents' divorce when I was 12 years old. My parents were social climbers. My mother was depressed and addicted to alcohol. My father was a gambler and addicted to other women.

Education was my salvation: If only I could get some higher degrees, I could somehow validate myself. Certainly, I had little chance to distinguish myself as an athlete or as a member of the most popular groups. I was an outcast, a loner who longed to be admired for something that separated me from the rest. It was not until well into my college years that I discovered that by achieving academically I could finally win the approval that I so desperately craved.

As a student, I learned my lessons with great difficulty. Through most of high school, I was both a behavior problem and a marginal student. Now, I am a teacher facing a roomful of kids who are like me and yet not like me at all.

I looked out across the room and wondered if we are from the same planet. It was as if the children were plugged into high-voltage electricity, vibrating with energy. The quietest among them was rhythmically bouncing her crossed leg to the sounds of music seeping out from beneath a cascade of hair, surreptitiously hiding the earphones. It was not that she cared that I saw the radio or not; it was just a game in which she was supposed to make an effort to be discreet.

I could not give much attention to her anyway. I had my hands full with the rest of her classmates, who were simmering and seething like a beehive that had just been kicked. I was trying to speak with them but I was fairly sure that I was talking only to myself.

I could see swatches of color spread throughout the room, as if a giant hand had reached in and dunked the kids into one of several buckets. The Asian contingent, which for some reason was composed mostly of girls, sat along the first row like a geometric stripe of glistening black hair that seemed to ripple from one head to next. Behind them sat a mixed assortment of cultural backgrounds—children of Irish, Italian, Hispanic, and generic white stock—as if they had taken their seats randomly. Further back, an invisible line seemed to divide the room, with white "jocks" occupying the left rows and a group of blacks on the right.

Along the further reaches of the territory, I could see still other cultures represented, but before I could begin to make sense of their identity my ears were bombarded by the sounds of half a dozen languages. I could hear Spanish being spoken in a staccato far too fast for me to understand. What I had first assumed was a homogeneous group of Chinese or Japanese students turned out to include a few Vietnamese, a few Hong Kong Chinese speaking Cantonese, and one Japanese exchange student speaking English to a Pacific Islander who was having as much trouble as I was understanding the words. I could hear the athletes talking "jock speak" and the blacks speaking in an "ebonic" dialect while the mixed group of academic achievers sitting in the middle were waiting patiently for class to begin, speaking loudly with their eyes. I looked out at this symphony of cultures, questioning how I could ever hope to reach all their different interests.

As this narrative clearly indicates, the culture within each of us becomes the filter by which we make sense of all that we experience and the means by which we relate to the cultures of all with whom we attempt to teach. It is a wonder that clear and constructive communication ever takes place between human beings, given our diversity. It is a miracle that we can teach anyone anything considering the unique ways in which we relate to the world and the conflicting agendas of each party concerned.

Cultural Values

Each of us has some very strong opinions about how education should best take place. Some among us believe quite strongly that what kids need most is strong and consistent discipline, clear expectations, structured activities, and immediate feedback on how they are performing. Others feel just as passionately that education best takes place when quite the opposite conditions occur—flexible boundaries, negotiable rules, relative autonomy, and an emphasis on self-assessment rather than on teacher input. Of course, there is evidence to indicate that both belief systems, and others in between, have some merit, depending on the setting, the goals, and the particular needs of the children.

We can look at assessment as another example of how personal values enter into a supposedly objective process. The idea of a "culture-free" method of assessing children's performance—one that is free of biases toward the majority—is patently absurd. Sowell (1994, p. 179) makes the point that "since there are no culture-free societies, all performances will be performance in some given culture."

Within the academic arena, in which intelligence is equated with abilities to read and compute numbers, disparities between various cultures have been repeatedly documented in which Chinese Americans consistently score highest and African Americans score lowest. When intelligence is defined as a kind of split-second decision making in which body and mind are coordinated in such a way to outcompete others to achieve a goal, however, there is quite a different outcome. Sowell (1994) questions if it is a coincidence that African Americans excel in fields such as basketball, the running back position in football, or jazz, in which improvisational decision making under pressure is required.

What is interesting to ponder is how this differential cultural excellence emerged. Genetic differences could certainly play a part but, just as likely, members of particular cultures are indoctrinated from birth into a particular discourse that programs them to focus on some areas rather than others. Our particular values related to education and teaching, as well, were shaped, in part, by training and supervision. We all read literature, studied research, engaged in dialogue with peers and mentors, and experimented with different approaches as part of our professional development. There are some very basic values, however, related not only to the classroom but also to our lives that were programmed long before we ever dreamed of being teachers.

Some of these strong beliefs we hold reflect our individually evolved preferences based on personality and even biological variables. For example, the fact that you enjoy doing things with children that are essentially physically, emotionally, or cognitively based could very well result from how your neurological system is wired. This may have less to do with your cultural upbringing than it does with your individual biological constitution that predisposes you to react in particular ways. In other words, we are products of not only culture but also evolution and physiology.

It is clear that other values we hold are very much influenced by our cultural background. The dimension of time is a good example. Traditionally, men and women have treated time differently, and this has been clearly evident in how men and women conduct their daily business. Although the boundaries between genders are becoming increasingly blurred, men have tended to be much more goal oriented, much more concerned with content rather than process, and much more concerned with getting things done within allotted time parameters. Within the culture of women, time is also considered useful when it is spent engaged in the pursuit of intimacy. Among men, however, time is often considered wasted if it is not spent contributing to the gross national product.

Gender is but one part of the culture within each of us that shaped our values related to time management (even that term reflects a value), and perhaps time perception related to education. Consider the relative importance that punctuality—that is, being on time—has in your life and in your classroom. Teachers spend an incredible amount of their own time dealing with absence and tardy reports—violations of time parameters in the school. The whole concept of time—its pace, boundaries, and meaning—is treated quite differently in various cultures.

For example, ordinarily very precise about time, I started a workshop 6 minutes late after the lunch break to allow for stragglers to get settled in. The audience was made up largely of people of German and Lutheran heritage, and the setting was a conservative, small city in the Midwest. When it came time to look over the course evaluations, it was apparent that quite a few participants were disturbed by the late (6 minutes!) starting time after lunch—enough so that they mentioned it in their comments even though they enjoyed the workshop.

I contrast this episode with one involving another group of students in a different culture within Latin America. I value punctuality more as a personal rather than a cultural value. Even for North Americans, who generally prize being on time as an important dimension of daily life (compared to other places), I am more fastidious than most. I hate to be kept waiting, so I do not make others wait. I am early for everything.

Therefore, if I have a 10:00 a.m. class, and especially in a first meeting when I want to make a good impression, I will be at my station in front of the room at precisely 9:55. This I did while meeting a group of students at an elite university in Peru.

When 10:00 rolled around, I looked around the room in panic to face rows of empty chairs. Surely I have been sitting in the wrong room, I thought in panic. Now I am going to be late for sure.

No such luck. This was the right room after all. At 10 minutes after the hour, a few students strolled casually into the room. "This is Educational Psychology?" I asked them in careful Spanish. I received only a look in return that said, "Why, of course!" I further asked them, "And what time was this class to begin?" They chattered among themselves for a moment, then ignored me to take their seats.

By 10:20, the room was half full and by 10:30 there was a quorum, although during the next half hour students would continue to trickle in, usually at the exact moment I was laboriously constructing my stilted Spanish descriptions of complex ideas that I was not certain I even understood in English. By 11:00, I was exhausted and decided it was time for a break. Big mistake.

I warned them, pleadingly, that because we got a very late start we will resume at precisely 11:15. "Esta claro?" Their solemn nods reassured me.

No doubt you have guessed the outcome. There I sat in an empty room until, at 11:30, a few students returned to face my interrogation.

I asked them, "Where have you all been? Wasn't I clear when I said we would begin at the appointed time? And where is everyone else?" I could not control my exasperation. "Quien sabe?" They shrugged and unconcernedly took their seats.

I was baffled by this situation but nevertheless finished the half-empty class. Because it was now lunch time, I headed over to the cafeteria for something to eat and to reflect on this disaster that had been my first teaching assignment in their culture. Lo and behold, as I walked into the restaurant, there sat my wayward class members deep in discussion over cups of coffee. I could not restrain my indignation as I approached their table.

"Where have you all been?" I sputtered, seeing quite clearly the answer to my feeble question was before me.

Their intense conversation abruptly stopped. One spokesperson addressed me in English, so there would be no misunderstanding: "Why Professor Kottler, we have been talking about the issues you raised in class. Is there some problem?"

I replied, "Ur, well, I couldn't help but notice you hadn't returned." Then, like a torrent, my frustration tumbled out: "Look, first you come to class, and the first class at that, a half hour late. No apologies. Not even an acknowledgment that your behavior was rude and insensitive. Then you didn't have the courtesy to even return after break."

They were as dumbfounded as I was. I could see it in their faces. Patiently and carefully, and in perfect English, the same student wondered why being on time was so important to me. Furthermore, why was it so crucial that they return to the classroom? Was it not clear that they were intensely involved in discussing the issues, not only beyond the walls of class but also by now far beyond the assigned time parameters? In fact, they were so absorbed in the subject, they intended to spend another hour or two together. Might I be interested in joining them?

Ever since that day, I have considered that between the German and Peruvian cultural values of time, each of us has a personal stake in that territory. Each child has a different association with time, an individualized construction of its meaning and relevance. This is no surprise to any teacher because he or she sees manifestations of these cultural differences every day, among not only various ethnic groups but also children of different genders, socioeconomic backgrounds, and every other microculture that could be named.

Culture as Individuality

In this chapter, I have shared a few examples of how the cultures within each of us become obstacles as well as gifts to understanding and relating to students from different backgrounds. I can think of a dozen examples in which I struggled with particular students, labeling them as "troublemakers," "unmotivated," "resistant," and "underachievers," because they did not fit my usual expectations for what is appropriate conduct in the classroom. On reflection, I now wonder about the extent to which their behavior resulted from, or at least was exacerbated by, the clash between our respective cultures. I did not understand them; they did not understand me. I was convinced that they were the problem—their laziness, insensitivity, or ignorance—just as they were equally certain that it was my rigidity, arrogance, and stupidity that created the problems between us.

It is humbling to consider the extent to which all learning that takes place in the classroom, or anywhere else for that matter, results in part from a respectful alignment between the cultures of all participants. Whether we are aware of it or not, our cultures are showing through in everything that we do. Our students are exquisitely sensitive to our moods, our values and beliefs, and our standards for excellence. They know when they are being judged. They can feel our disapproval no matter what steps we take to pretend that we care.

When we stand before children, droning on about some aspect of language, history, or beauty that we consider important, we often look like creatures from another planet to them. In a sense, we are. The values of our culture are, in many ways, completely different from those of our students.

It is important, as well, to avoid the kind of separatist mentality that focuses on dividing people into discrete groups, in much the same way that I have already done so when contrasting small-town Lutherans with urban Peruvians in their concepts of time. Culture is not about a group identity but rather about an individual identity. Education takes place as a series of ongoing social interactions among unique individuals and not between their cultural groups.

In the chapters that follow, I encourage you to move beyond reliance on group-focus orientations that confuse people with their cultural labels. I challenge you to begin thinking about students as having unique cultures that are always showing, just like your own.

Climate of
Political Correctness

For all practical purposes, it is one of the greatest secrets of our time—spoken about in whispers to those we trust, mumbled to ourselves during times of stress, and even spoken about openly with the right group around. I am referring to what many teachers really think and feel about all the attention to multicultural diversity.

If we placed recording devices in teachers' lounges around the country or, for that matter, any staff room in which professionals gather to relax and let their guards down, we would most likely hear a number of private conversations that are hardly ever spoken publicly, including the following:

> I think this stuff is all a fad, just like hula hoops. Every few years we get another order about what we should all be doing. I think professors who haven't seen a classroom in a decade sit around and make up ideas—they call it research— that they sell to somebody in power. That's what all this

multidimensional crap is all about—something that liberal
do-gooders at the university think will get them tenure if
they can get us to be in their experiments. Meanwhile, the
kids keep getting more violent and uncooperative.

There is indeed a public image of political correctness that is
projected to the world by most teachers: that we are fair and decent,
that we embrace the diversity of our students and faculty, and that
we are free of prejudices and biases, committed only to doing the best
jobs we can. This is the same mandate we were taught (publicly) by
our instructors and supervisors, the same one found in our texts and
now in the weekly messages that come from the Multicultural Diversity Office in the district, and the same rah-rah speech we hear (again
publicly) from administrators and the school board.

"Cultural diversity is good" proclaims the union spokespeople.
"Multiculturalism is our greatest strength" the politicians tell us.
Every news anchor or legal team, television show, and even commer-
cials have that perfect blend of skin colors represented to show that
they are culturally sensitive—for example, "We follow affirmative
action" and "We are responsive to the demographics of our view-
ers—see, one white person, one African American, one Mexican
American, one Asian American, and someone of mixed race to satisfy
everyone else."

The 1995-1996 calendar published by the California Teachers
Association listed the following memorable "Dates to Remember":
Internment of Japanese Americans Day (February 19), the birthday
of Mahavira, the founder of Jainism (April 30), Stonewall Rebellion
Anniversary (June 27), National Coming Out Day (October 11), and
Massacre of the Sioux at Wounded Knee Day (December 29). No
wonder there is cynicism among teachers. No wonder teachers sometimes go through the motions of doing what is mandated without
any real passion or conviction for the underlying messages.

One Slip and You Are Under Arrest!

My how things have changed! The *Washington Post* mentioned
the term *politically correct* within its pages only 9 times during the
year 1987. Seven years later, a sampling of this newspaper, which
perhaps best reflects our times, showed that the term was used 292

times (Morley, 1995). The term *political correctness* was originally intended to help reverse cultural trends toward racism and sexism through self-consciously civil language (used in public, anyway). It is generally defined as "good manners" or "appropriate social behavior," although novelist Saul Bellow once described it as "free speech without debate."

Echoing Bellow's sentiment, Radosh (1993) stated at a symposium on the subject of multiculturalism and political correctness that this issue is actually a threat to the integrity of our culture. He cites the following examples to support his argument that the multicultural movement has gotten so out of control that we have lost all perspective on what is important:

1. The Baltimore Board of Education paid a consultant an exorbitant fee to develop a compulsory Afrocentric curriculum for the children of the state. When queried as to whether teaching children that Ancient Egypt was a black African culture was accurate, the response was that it does not really matter; history is filled with distortions. Why not slant things in the other direction for a change?

2. The District of Columbia Board of Education hired their own consultant—a woman who created her own "university" and then awarded herself a degree from that institution so she would have necessary credentials. She then developed a program, later approved by the superintendent, that promoted self-esteem through Afrocentric languages and arts rather than addressing the standard curriculum of mathematics, American history, world events, and so on.

3. At Wellesley College, a professor of African studies was allowed to use anti-Semitic literature to teach students that Jews were responsible for not only the slave trade but also the extermination of all Native Americans. Radosh wonders if a Jewish professor using Ku Klux Klan literature in class would be similarly tolerated.

4. At Hampshire College, two professors with exemplary records were repeatedly denied tenure by the president because they insisted on teaching European literature in their classes instead of the mandated Third World curriculum.

5. On the release of his film *Malcolm X*, Spike Lee announced that he would give interviews to only African American journal-

ists because only they could understand the meaning of his work.

In battling what he sees as censorship, oppression, and power plays by the disenfranchised, Kramer (1993) concurs with the assessment that any dissent or disagreement about issues related to cultural diversity is cast as racist, sexist, or homophobic. One further case in point gained notoriety because of the extent to which the original incident spinned out of control. Francis Lawrence, president of Rutgers State University, was reported to have said in an address to faculty that minority students have difficulty passing standardized exams because of genetic limitations. This single phrase in a 2-hour rambling speech, a single minute in a 30-year career, all but destroyed his reputation.

Strikes by students closed down a scheduled athletic event. Other students boycotted the classes of anyone who even dared come to his defense. Many students, faculty, and members of the community called for his resignation because of his perceived insensitivity at best and racism at worst. End of case.

Or is it?

Further investigations by the *New York Times* and *U.S. News and World Report* (Leo, 1995a) discovered that quite a different picture emerged of this supposed racist administrator. As it turns out, there was a context for his remarks that, although inexcusable, may at least be comprehensible. Lawrence had been rambling for almost 2 hours—well past the lunch hour—when he bumbled. He had just repudiated the best-selling book *The Bell Curve* as morally wrong for implying there were genetic characteristics that make certain minority groups less intellectually capable. In fact, he had been in the middle of giving an impassioned politically correct tirade on the importance of cultural diversity when he garbled his sentence.

Even those who believe that this (Freudian?) slip was inexcusable must still consider his previous record. While vice president at Tulane University, he was responsible for raising the minority representation among students and faculty on campus from 1% to 10%. His current institution is a "shrine" to multiculturalism, with new programs he implemented such as a speech code, diversity awareness training, and ethnic affirming environments in the residence halls. Unfortunately, "multiculturalism has evolved into a harsh faith, strong on punishment and eager to monitor isolated phrases for signs of heresy" (Leo, 1995b, p. 22).

Whether Francis Lawrence is a closet racist or not and whether his blunder was an unconscious expression of true convictions or a lapse in concentration is not the point. His case has come to symbolize for many the excesses of the thought and speech police: One slip and you are under arrest.

A counterpoint offered by Frye (1992) laments that the term *politically correct* can no longer be uttered without some irony, implying righteous bullying, faddish opinions, and snotty pride. Proud of being both "political" and "correct," or at least striving for correctness, Frye hotly debates critics who would disparage efforts to create greater equality for all. Indeed, without affirmative action programs, civil rights laws, political demonstrations, and, yes, revision of our cultural values and public language, rampant inequities between genders and among various ethnic groups would be even greater.

Nevertheless, throughout history, and throughout the world, there have been inequities between cultures in which those in power attempt to control, if not exploit, those who are powerless. This may not be morally right, but it has been the way of our race since the beginning of time. That is why it takes such extraordinary efforts on our part to reverse a half million years of oppression.

That the Poor and Weak Shall Wither

In most every society in the world, both now and in the past, there is a division of population based on economic resources. This differential accumulation of wealth can be determined by birth, such as in the case of royal families versus serfs, or it may be the result of some people having more ability than others. There is no doubt that there are some individuals who are brighter and more ambitious, talented, and ruthless than others. There is also an unlevel playing field with regard to kin relations and networking bonds that provide more opportunities for some people rather than others.

We can lament the problems of poverty all we want and cry out against the injustice of the rich having so much more than the poor, but unfortunately it has always been that way among humankind.

In fact, even among animals, there is hardly an equal distribution of food among all members. Those who are the most fierce or well connected receive more than their fair share. Even bees and ants are born as a slave, middle manager, or queen.

Evolutionists see no problem with this state of affairs. It is the way of the world that the fittest should survive while the weak should wither. Education is one way that society controls who shall flourish and who shall not. Because it is the means by which we prepare the young for survival in the world, whether the primarily valued skills are hunting antelope, capturing turtles, diving for pearls, or writing grammatically correct essays, it has always made sense that members of the ruling class would have the best training and opportunities. After all, it has been reasoned for millennia, why waste the precious resource of structured education on the masses when the best and brightest could profit most? Even if this class division is not based on ability or merit, why on earth should those in control allow others to usurp them and the right of their children to enjoy the choicest opportunities?

That class divisions in most cultures are based on racial characteristics is hardly a coincidence, nor is it the result of differential aptitude. It is not that whites are more capable than blacks in South Africa or on our own continent; merely that the ruling class has had access to greater resources and better educational opportunities. It is also a human pattern that we tend to help others who are like us, who are members of our identified tribe, while scorning others who are different.

What is unprecedented in human history is the relatively recent attempts to provide more equal educational opportunities to all children regardless of the socioeconomic class to which they were born. Of course, the concept of true equal opportunity in our schools is a myth. We could visit any urban school system and find that more privileged areas have far more resources, nicer facilities, and better teachers than those in economically disadvantaged areas. Kozol (1991) described all too poignantly how, in one typical urban school system (Chicago), 60% of the children drop out of school prior to graduation. Of those who do manage to finish high school, only a tiny fraction ever read well enough to succeed in college. A staggering 97% of students attending the city's community colleges never finish their studies. Turning his attention to New York City, Kozol discovered that three times as much money was spent per pupil in suburban versus city schools.

Compared to a mere generation ago when it would have been unheard of to offer public education to all children of every station in life, however, the current educational policy is downright revolutionary. What this means for us as teachers, however, is that we must deal with an increasingly diverse student population. Sitting in class next to one another are some students who can have everything they have ever dreamed of and others who dream only of a new pair of shoes.

The class evolution for teachers has changed as well in recent years. No matter how much we complain about being ridiculously underpaid, we are all firmly entrenched in the middle class. We own homes and cars and can afford (modest) vacations.

This is not the case for teachers in other parts of the world where a vow of poverty is often expected along with the commitment to education. Whereas in our culture teachers belong to a class that is higher than that of some students and lower than that of others, in many parts of Asia teachers may enjoy a certain respect but may also reside on the lowest rung of the economic ladder. What this means is that teachers in our culture do not identify most strongly with the poorest children but rather with children similar to themselves. Therefore, we may allow the underclasses entrance into our educational system and tell them they can make it on their own abilities, but they certainly do not have nearly the potential and resources to succeed.

Motivation surely plays a key role. To children of the upper or middle class, education is clearly perceived as a means to become upwardly mobile. From the earliest age, such children are admonished to do well in school if they are ever to amount to anything. To children of the lower class, however, education is not valued nearly as much, and this is a situation that mainstream cultures have not been very interested in changing.

Tribal Wars

If we are honest, all this is about control over resources. It has been the history of our species that those in positions of power would ensure that people of their own kind receive the largest share of meat, the choicest property, and the best positions. This is, after all, what many multiculturalists argue: that white middle class is the mainstream culture and, like any group that is in control, its members seek to impose their values on others. Even though this has been the way of things for hundreds of thousands of years—that the dominant culture enforces its will on minority cultures within the community—this is not necessarily the morally correct position to take.

By and large, we are tribal creatures drawn to those who share our skin color, ethnicity, religious convictions, and, most of all, genetic material. It is among our most natural drives to do our best to help those who are part of our group to the exclusion of others who are different.

Human beings have been killing each other since the beginning of time simply because they are not of the same tribe: Assyrians versus Babylonians, Romans versus Carthaginians, Moors versus Spaniards, Boers versus the English, Iroquois versus Algonquins, Paiutes versus Utes, Croats versus Serbs, Turks versus Armenians, Japanese versus Koreans, Peruvians versus Ecuadorians, Hutu versus Tutsi, Khmer Rouge versus Cambodians, Irish Catholics versus Protestants, Union versus the Confederacy, Bloods versus Crips, Arabs versus Jews, Romans versus Christians, Montagues versus Capulets, and Hatfields versus McCoys. The list goes on and on.

Although we have been shocked by the murder of 6 million Jews during the Holocaust, there have been twice that many deaths since then by members of one racial group trying to obliterate another (Horowitz, 1985). In the past four decades, there have been at least 25 documented cases of systematic genocide, including several claiming victims numbering in the hundreds of thousands, including Bangladesh, Cambodia, Bosnia, Sudan, Indonesia, Burundi, and Uganda. Humans are not alone in their propensity to wage wars of extermination toward those of different tribes. Ants, lions, chimpanzees, gorillas, wolves, and hyenas will kill off rival colonies that compete for their territories.

There is a natural tendency for us to expend our time, energy, and resources in the service of those who are like us, who most share our genes. According to evolutionary psychology, all human action can be examined in terms of its likelihood of helping an individual perpetuate his or her gene pool (Wright, 1994). Because there are limited resources available, whether that is translated into the best food or teaching materials, it is in your own best interests to help others most like you and to sabotage those who are most different. Anything that is attained by someone of a competing tribe is often at your expense.

This is why we are so enamored by our spectator sports. Students (and teachers) will scream their hearts out in support of their team over a rival school's team. Soccer fans from one city in Italy will literally kill those from another because they support different tribal gladiators. Whether in football, basketball, rugby, or tennis, symbolically we are paying others to fight our battles and to conquer others who are members of another tribe.

Tribal affiliations most naturally evolve among those who share similar racial features (ethnicity), genetic material (family), economic goals (socioeconomic class), and value systems (religion). If you look around at who you trust the most, who your friends are, and who you spend the most time with, you will notice that your own tribal affiliations have particular characteristics. They may be based on shared preferences and interests, on similar goals and aspirations, or perhaps on "traditional" demarcations that include culture. In any case, your tribe is held together not only by what you have in common and what you are for but also by what you are against. There may be a friendly rivalry between first-floor versus second-floor lunch groups, between the social studies versus the science faculties, between the Methodists and the Lutherans, or between the younger teachers and those who are veterans, but there is, nevertheless, some conflict between the tribes.

Am I saying that multicultural harmony is futile and that embracing diversity is hopeless given our selfish genetic motives and tribal inclinations? Difficult, yes. Impossible, hardly.

What I am advocating is that there are very powerful reasons why we feel some degree of resentment toward people of cultures different from our own profiting at our expense. Every federal dollar that is spent in the inner cities of Detroit and Chicago is at the expense of those in rural Montana or Nevada. Every new extended education program designed to reach children in sparsely populated areas is at the expense of other resources that could be allocated to children in urban areas. Every moment of extra attention that we give to a disadvantaged child trying to catch up is at the expense of the economically advantaged child seeking enrichment.

No wonder this whole subject of multiculturalism is so hotly debated. What is at stake is no less than a distribution of monies, services, and resources to particular groups rather than other groups. Who is most deserving? Who do we owe the most? Who will make the most noise if they are left out? Most of all, who is most like us?

Politics of Victimization

In our "culture of complaint," Hughes (1993) writes about the victim-as-hero mentality that has become all pervasive. We should all have something or someone to blame for why we are not getting what we want or what we deserve in life. Hughes states that "Complaint gives you power—even when it's only the power of emotional bribery, of creating previously unnoticed levels of social guilt" (p. 9). Depending on your community, you have to stand alone to feel abused and to reap the benefits of being a protected group that is entitled to special treatment. In Seattle or San Francisco, transsexuals are considered a protected group, whereas in New Orleans it is French Acadians, in Cincinnati it is those of Appalachian origin, in Pasadena it is Armenian Americans, and in Massachusetts it is Portuguese immigrants. Bankers, Canadian Americans, Italian Americans, and, in fact, all people are members of some protected minority, whether that is related to their age, religious beliefs, skin color, sexual orientation, ancestry, gender, or marital status.

In the classroom, there is a similar culture of complaint in which students' unacceptable or irresponsible behavior is never their fault but rather the result of some injustice: "It's not my fault I don't have my homework" is a familiar refrain. "Whose fault is it then?" we wonder aloud.

Of course, there are a staggering number of possibilities, including the following:

"My mother forgot to wake me in time."
"Because my parents were disadvantaged, they couldn't help me with it."
"I had to babysit for my family."
"You weren't clear about what you wanted."
"Nobody in my family ever did well in school."

"I *did* my homework but if I give it to you I am just
contributing to the class struggle between the 'haves' and
'have-nots.' "

Lest we become too smug, it is not unusual for teachers to also
resort to the same blaming strategies as to why they are not the way
they prefer. For example,

"How can I teach these kids when they don't even try?"
"The district doesn't support us so how am I supposed to do
my job?"
"The damn administrators are always discovering new ways
to sabotage my efforts. There is no sense in even trying
anymore."
"It's the parents—How can I do my job if they won't do
theirs?"
"I just don't have supportive colleagues. I can't be expected to
do it all alone."
"With how little they pay me, no wonder I'm not all that
motivated.'
"These kids are just going back to their same old
neighborhoods and gangs."

Of course, these are good excuses—quite legitimate reasons
why things are not as we would like them to be. In the politics of
being a victim, however, you receive the following benefits (J. Kottler,
1994):

1. *You are able to disown responsibility for the problems.* After all, it
   is not your fault. If only the students/parents/adminis-
   trators/other teachers/legislators would act differently, then
   you would not have these difficulties.
2. *You get to stay stuck and do not have to invest the greater time and
   energy it would take to change things.* Because it is all but hopeless, there is no sense in you working harder to make a
   difference. You might as well accept the status quo and complain about how tough things are.

3. *You get pity from others (and can feel sorry for yourself) for being so misunderstood and unappreciated.* You are able to revel in the role of being a victim.

Whether you are a student, a teacher, or in any other role in life, being a victim is empowering in how you can manipulate other people to rescue you. The message comes through at the most primitive levels of moral reasoning: Help the disadvantaged not because it is right or because it is fair but because we owe them for past injustices. What is not stated is that unless we do address the problems of poverty, crime, and despair among the underclasses, they will take what they want, feeling they have nothing else to lose.

Some Questionable Assumptions

One of the reasons there is so much cynicism and distrust directed toward the multicultural movement is that perceived fairness is sacrificed in lieu of policies that appear to be based on special interests of particular groups that happen to be the most fashionable victims of popular guilt. Multiculturalism has become, in the words of Schlesinger (1992), a "multiethnic dogma" in which assimilation and integration are replaced by fragmentation and separatism.

Recently, one primary goal of education has been to celebrate, if not perpetuate, ethnic identities—a kind of segregation Schlesinger (1992) believes will only lead to greater antagonism and competition between groups. The bonds between children of different races are being weakened, leading to a greater "tribalization" of North American life. The primary assumption of the multicultural movement, that of respecting the differences among diverse peoples, has actually changed from a reaction against Eurocentrism into a kind of ethnocentrism of its own—one that refers only to non-Western, nonwhite cultures.

There are a number of other assumptions on which this movement is built that make neither intuitive sense nor are they supported by research evidence. The following is a sampling of these operating principles:

Blending is better than separating people. Given a choice, people of particular cultures prefer to live and work with members of their own tribe. Observe any school cafeteria, playground, or teachers' lounge and there is better than an even chance that coalitions are based less on shared interests and more on skin color, ethnic origins, and religious preferences.

Structures and institutions derived from Western Europe are oppressive and racist, whereas those derived from Third World and indigenous cultures are not. In fact, there is considerable evidence that once any group becomes the majority, with corresponding power and influence, those not in power will suffer deprivation of resources and opportunities. Even within minority cultures, there are social hierarchies that allocate status and privilege based on skin color, parental lineage, spoken accents, and chosen line of work. Prejudices by the majority culture are racism, but among minority cultures such beliefs are considered legitimate self-protection.

Diversity is conducive to interesting and productive growth in culture. Actually, there is evidence that the opposite is true. Multiethnic groups are conducive to destabilization of a society. The old Soviet Union dissolved, in part, because of irreconcilable squabbles between their tribes, whereas homogeneity in Japan makes it far easier to manage social behavior. In the United States, which is affectionately labeled a "melting pot" of cultures, there is far more fractionalization and civil disputes than would be the case if the country consisted of a single background.

The contributions of each culture and language should be given equal legitimacy. This assumption leads us to give equal weight to various cultures, regardless of their proportion of representation in the community or even of their relative merits in the daily world. Thus, Swahili should be offered as much as Spanish, or Che Guevara is as important a historical figure as Thomas Jefferson.

History should be rewritten to reflect a new reality. This new order is one in which Columbus was a blood-crazed opportunist, on a par with Hitler, for his slaughter of native people. Indigenous peoples of America were living in peaceful coexistence prior to European invasion. Rather than bent on brutal warfare and the systematic destruction of neighboring tribes, they lived in harmony with nature. This is pure fabrication. Actually, what one tribe did to another was just as brutal, if not more so, than anything Europeans tried. The major difference, however, is that, with guns, European immigrants were simply more efficient than the Sioux in subjugating other tribes.

Another example of historical inaccuracies that are politically correct is the idea that Europeans introduced slavery to Africa. Actually, the term *slavery* was a Muslim invention. The word *slave* originates from the subjugation of Slavic Caucasians who were sold throughout the Muslim world. Also, it cannot be both ways: If history is now being rewritten in such a way that Egypt is considered to have been a black African culture, then it was also a brutal nation that enslaved Jews to run its economy.

The myths perpetuated by Afrocentrism are as dangerous and dishonest as any other form of "centrism" that distorts truth in lieu of more useful views of history. Writing about the intellectual condescension toward the people it is purported to aid, Will (1996) cites examples of revisionist history that claim Plato developed his philosophy in Africa, Beethoven was Afro-European, and Napoleon destroyed the Sphinx's nose because of its resemblance to African features, even though there is not the slightest shred of evidence to support these claims.

In his attempts to empower African Americans, Will (1996) writes that these inspiring myths actually teach people to alter reality according to their own preferences—a strategy not exactly useful in the long run. How can such ideas have legitimacy if they do not follow the most rudimentary rules of objective inquiry?

As a counterpart to these arguments, Bassey (1993) points out that all realities are embedded in culturally convenient distortions. No doubt Eurocentric history is slanted as well, especially in such a way that certain inconvenient facts that portray the mainstream culture in an unfavorable light are ignored.

Cultural identity is a static, fixed state—one that is recognizable by skin color or language spoken. African American or Mexican American middle-class professionals often have values more in common with others in their suburban neighborhoods and office building than they do with other members of their own race or ethnic background. Class is often a better predictor of similarity than race.

One of the unintended consequences of the multicultural movement has been the tendency to assume that individuals of a particular color, race, religion, class, or geographical location are basically the same. Thus, lower-class African American urban residents are presumed to have certain characteristics that are different from small-town rural Lutherans or Cuban American Republicans from Miami. The truth is that members of particular groups often do share attributes in common, whether they are certain physical features, an historical legacy, or culturally programmed tastes in food, fashion, or music.

As much as members of particular cultural groups hold in common, gross generalizations lead to a number of misconceptions. In some cases, the differences within groups are greater than those between them. In other words, the result of constantly emphasizing a person's culture is that in the process that person's individuality may be lost. There develops a different kind of racism, one well intended but that nevertheless makes assumptions about people because of their skin color, gender, or religious convictions. We are not sure what sense to make of a conservative Republican black man who abhors affirmative action. We find it just as jarring to encounter anyone who does not fit our stereotypes—an upper-class Presbyterian who becomes a delinquent or a captain of the football team who happens to be gay.

Emphasizing our differences is better than emphasizing our commonalities. First and foremost, we are all human beings with a shared stake in this planet. Next, we are citizens of nations, with all the pride and rigidity associated with the beliefs that we are far better than others across an imaginary line in the sand.

There are too many lines in the educational sands of our schools today; they separate, discriminate, and fractionalize students from one another. Tracking, for example, offers some students "higher-level" classes. Just hanging around a teachers' lounge will show very quickly and clearly how tracking causes teachers to focus on differences between students rather than their commonalities. As a general rule, the most experienced teachers get the upper academic tracks, and the rookies, just fresh out of school, are assigned the lower-functioning student groups.

If any institution is to be blamed for perpetuating separateness and cultural discrimination, it is our public schools. Lest you doubt this, ask yourself the following question: Between 1st and 12th grades, what do students learn about themselves relative to their peers after spending all that time being tested, labeled, grouped, graded, honored, and dishonored? Cultural separatism is a way of school life. If there is one thing that students learn in school, it is how very different they are from others who come from a different social class or academic track.

Perhaps it is a case of envy and jealousy on my part. I was not very successful as a student in my early years. When my friends were in chemistry, I was in shop class. When they were in honors English and science, I muddled along with the rest of the masses in the average-level classes. It never occurred to me that I might be smart, that I might have anything going for me, and that I might have potential to be successful. After all, tests showed that I was of average intelligence. My grades indicated that I was a marginal student. Even my parents believed I would be lucky to get into a college, much less ever graduate.

These class divisions are initiated by school administrators and also enforced by the various cultures among the children themselves. Each of us can remember our own school days and the rigid social hierarchy that existed among various groups: cheerleaders and jocks in one group, but even this had its popular and marginal subgroups depending on what position you played, your physical appearance, and perceived popularity; rich kids in another group, ranked according to the location of your house, the status of your parents' cars, the size of your allowance, and the labels on your wardrobe; working-class white kids in another group, divided into its own territory according to physical size and strength and other factors too numerous to mention; the same with the Asian kids, the Hispanic kids, and the black kids; and the nerds, divided among themselves according to their grade point averages and the number of honors classes they were taking. The whole school is a complex cross-categorization of people.

More Alike Than Different

Ethnic festivals and restaurants, cultural pride days, and so on celebrate our unique lineages. By always stressing our differences, however, we also exacerbate tribal conflicts. Educational movements to provide Afrocentric or feminist curricula are designed to empower and instill pride in marginalized groups, but they can also further alienate peoples. Some would say, "Fine, this is war." For our common culture to work, however, we must be able to speak a universal language, not only in spoken words but also in the shared symbols and history. The current discourse surrounding multiculturalism is, then, a negotiation between those who have been in power (mostly heterosexual males of European, Protestant descent) and those who would like more power, particularly with regard to future agendas. If our cultural symbols, language, and history are truly to be shared by all, then they have to be constructed in such a way that all of us can recognize a part of what we hold most sacred.

There can indeed be a compromise between respect for cultural differences and the need for cultural unity. How interesting our classrooms have become with the influx of children who bring a rich assortment of backgrounds. How supportive these environments can be for those who have felt on the outside.

I teach a group of honors students in a seminar on freedom and identity. Varied in their interests and career goals, what they have in common is a record of academic achievement. Despite their school successes, they strike me as remarkably wounded. I notice that most of them will not say much in class. They seem timid and shy. When pressed as to why it is so difficult for many of them to speak up, one student explained:

> Even though we are supposed to be so smart, we are afraid to say something stupid, and when we do talk, we have rehearsed the words in our minds over and over. If I don't say anything I don't risk changing people's impressions.

Eventually, haltingly, they begin to talk, to tell their stories of how they ended up where they are now. As I listen to their narratives, I am struck not only by the diversity of their cultures but also by the disproportionate amount of pain they have suffered.

A Mexican American tells of being sexually abused by her father. A Cambodian refugee talks about how her mother was forced to watch her whole family murdered before her eyes. A Chinese immigrant was abandoned by her mother who returned to the old country to be with her lover. A Greek immigrant talks about being ostracized in high school for beating out others for valedictorian. An Italian American describes the emotional abuse she suffered by her father who would tease her for being fat and then sabotage her efforts to lose weight. A Japanese American shares her secret of living in poverty and of being afraid to bring friends home. A small-town young man tells his story of being overly attached to his parents, unable to let go. Another Mexican American talks about life with a father who was chronically depressed and suicidal. An ex-athlete explains how he came to be physically disabled. An urban kid describes how his father was killed trying to stop an armed robbery. A white student describes growing up on an Indian reservation, suffering discrimination because she was different. A Mormon responds sheepishly about how sheltered she has been and how hard it is for her to relate to these life experiences. Another student pipes in with his story of being an ex-gang member and drug addict. A chorus of others then jump in with similar stories—one young woman who was a "speed freak" and another who is an alcoholic. A Taiwanese American apologizes because she knows nothing about her language and culture. Last of all, an upper-middle-class white student says that he has a culture of his own that he would like others to understand and appreciate.

This is just one classroom of 20 students! Every one of us, and every one of our students, has a story to tell. I hope this classroom just described has more than its fair share of wounded students, but it nevertheless illustrates the sheer diversity of experiences. What is most significant about this group, however, is not their cultural differences, or even their varied traumas, but rather how they have come together to support one another. For the first time in their lives, these kids do not feel so alone. They feel part of something bigger than themselves. They feel like there is some place they belong—a shared culture they have built with one another.

Scapegoats

Political correctness does not treat all children equally. Depending on the climate of the times, some cultures become less equal than others. We take turns selecting particular cultural groups to denigrate. One week it may be the illegal immigrants slipping over the border from Mexico. The next week it might be Cambodian refugees or Haitian boat people. The powerless and homeless are not the only ones selected; even the wealthy of particular groups may be singled out—for example, Japanese corporations or Hong Kong Chinese who are buying up our most cherished properties.

Recently, it is the underclass that is taking its turn being flogged—more particularly, black inner-city mothers on welfare. As Wente (1995) points out, they are a perfect cultural subgroup to call the enemy. Because most people, and certainly most politicians, rarely come into contact with members of this culture, hidden as they are in a part of the city where few would dare to tread, there is little risk of a backlash. Welfare moms do not even vote, politicians reason, so there is little to fear there as well.

Mothers on welfare are thus portrayed as being morally unscrupulous and lacking character. Heck, they do not work, smoke crack all day, and sleep with an endless succession of men who will not even stick around to be a father to their children. Then we are stuck footing the bill, subsidizing this virtual crime factory called a ghetto. So goes the hysterical rantings of politicians seeking re-election and talk show hosts feeding the public frenzy for a scapegoat to which we can direct our anger.

Just as there is a fashion industry regarding clothing styles, best-selling books, and hit television shows, there is also a cultural fashion about which groups are in and which are out. Whereas once the Irish or Polish were considered the scapegoats, there has been a wide assortment of others who have slipped into that role—Jews, Lebanese, Japanese, Puerto Ricans, Chinese, Laotians, Filipinos, Mexicans, Cubans, and Haitians. The list goes on and on.

When the majority culture starts imitating particular minority cultures—for example, wearing baseball hats turned around, baggy shorts, or shaved heads—then a particular culture attains a degree of status, launching another search for a race to be defiled.

Reversing 100,000 Years
of History

The following is the major dilemma: Throughout history the prerogative of the winners has been to impose their will on the losers. Those who control the resources, the weapons and armies, and the economic base—in other words, those with power—have been the ones who have enjoyed the greatest benefits in a given culture. Although usually it is the majority of citizens who impose their will on the minorities in terms of dominant language and customs (e.g., the former Soviet Union or the United States), a very small minority group may control all others through control of weapons, political positions, and wealth (e.g., South Africa).

In the United States, as well as in many other Western nations, the so-called winners have been Caucasians. This is the group that has been the majority, in terms of sheer numbers, and controlled positions of power and influence. They have been the ones with the will, and the means to enforce this agenda, to write the history of the nation, to impose laws, and to decide who gets to sit in the front of the bus and who has the greatest opportunities for education and employment. Although this is not morally right, until now that has been beside the point: That is how the world works: I win, you lose, so I get to do what I want; or, there are more of us than you, so we get our way. You don't like it? Tough.

Whites signed treaties with Native Americans and then decided, "Hey, we won, forget those agreements. We can do what we want. Besides, what can you do about it?" Whites enslaved Africans and then, when Africans were freed, whites assigned them the lowest steps on the ladder of opportunity.

Once slavery was abolished, whites permitted immigration so they could have another cheap source of labor to exploit. Chinese were brought in to build the railroads. Irish were allowed in to take the urban jobs nobody else wanted. Mexicans were allowed to slip across the border to pick lettuce or apples but then were given few rights afforded the majority.

Is this right? Of course not. It has been the way of the world, however—until now.

For one of the few times in human history, the dominant culture is being forced to share its wealth and opportunities with those who have been shoved aside. These changes did not come about because of a higher level of moral reasoning, or even out of collective guilt, but rather because it had become evident that the so-called majority was outflanked and even increasingly outnumbered. Unless whites share the power, and continue to do so, civil war may very well be the result.

It is interesting to contemplate how various nations of the world are struggling in different ways with the reversal of history in which power is shared. Compare Australia and New Zealand, for example. They are two countries in the same geographical region that share similar stock of British immigrants. They have radically different policies and attitudes toward their indigenous peoples, however.

In Australia, the Aboriginals live on reservations or in urban ghettos (not unlike the situation among Native Americans). They are not a part of the majority culture in any sense. They hold little political power and do not have much social influence; only 4% of their population ever attend postsecondary education. They mostly keep to themselves, which seems fine with everyone else. Racism is as rampant in this country as it is anywhere in South Africa. With the high rates of infant mortality, premature adult death, poverty, unemployment, alcoholism, suicide, murder, deaths in police custody, and self-mutilation, Hazelhurst (1994) labels this as a form of genocide—an attempt to wipe this 50,000-year-old culture off the face of the Earth.

In New Zealand, however, quite a different cultural phenomenon has unfolded. English geographical names are reverting back to their historical Maori labels. Fishing rights and traditional native lands are being returned to their original Maori families. The Maori language is encouraged, if not required to some degree, for all school children. All governmental stationery proclaims both English and Maori headings. New Zealand prides itself, in fact, on its biculturalism.

Even though there are significant grumblings by members of the *Pakeha* (the Maori name for the majority culture), the government has been spearheading a movement to share power, lands, and resources with a minority, indigenous culture that does not have the means by which to take what they want. Like in North America, they first asked politely to have their lands returned to them. Next, they tried to negotiate and to appeal to the courts. Then, they resorted to violent opposition, rebellion, and civil disobedience. Even with considerable determination, it is not as if the Maoris or Native Americans could force the majority culture to share its power. They have had to find a way to appeal to the moral rightness of their positions. We live in a time, one of the few in human history, in which across the globe dominant cultures of particular nations are being cajoled, blackmailed, coerced, or persuaded (choose your preferred verb) to equalize the power in such a way that all people can share in the resources available, regardless of whether their ancestors won the last war.

With this unprecedented movement afoot, naturally there are growing pains. Just as minority cultures have complained over and over again that they want equal opportunities, now members of the majority culture are complaining about their power base eroding.

For every opportunity afforded the child of one disadvantaged group, there is one less option for the children of the ruling class. This is only part of the discussions that are whispered in the teachers' lounge. After all, in a sense, as teachers we have joined this ruling class. We may not wield much power in terms of economic clout, but we sure influence the minds of the next generation.

Just How Different
Are We, Anyway?

Throughout *What's Really Said in the Teachers' Lounge,* and in our larger culture, there has been a consistent focus on how each of us is so different. The historical legacy of our continent is that we are rugged individualists, fiercely independent, resenting the slightest attempts to control our rights to live where we want and keep as many guns as we need to feel safe.

One of the central values of North American culture has always been the sanctity of the individual to pursue happiness (within certain limits). Now, we are stressing yet another value: the importance of group distinctions. Every form we fill out asks us about our ethnic identification or our religious preference. Each of us has typed ourselves, or been classified by others, as members of a special tribe or breed, each with its own secret handshake. We are Methodists, Catholics, Buddhists, or Jews. We are city dwellers, suburbanites, residents of small towns, or hermits. We divide ourselves by class, profession, gender, education, political party, or even the organizations to which we feel allegiance—for example, the National Rifle

Association or the Sierra Club. We come in a rainbow of colors—brown, black, white, red, yellow, and every color in between.

There are even very subtle markers of racial identity within groups based on nuances of pigmentation. We speak of ethnicity as if we have but one; most of us are hybrids—mutts—of mixed culture. In the last national census, more than 300 races were represented by checking the box "other" and there were 600 different Indian tribes, 70 Hispanic groups, and a virtually unlimited number of combinations that might include Cherokee/Thai/Tongan/Irish American or African American/Welsh/Puerto Rican/Russian.

Writer Russell Baker (1994) asks, "To which tribe does a white person belong?" Being called a "WASP" is offensive. "Whitey" will not do either. Regarding the most formal term often used, Baker (p. 25) states the following: "My own tribe, I noticed while browsing in the press the other day, is being called 'Caucasian.' This is absurd. The Caucasus is a region between the Caspian and Black Seas and contains Russians, Georgians, Azerbaijanis, and Armenians." Baker, however, who is part Irish and part Cuban, laments that his tribe has no name.

As Schlesinger (1992) and other proponents of the "melting pot" conception of our nation lament, all this focus on human differences has the cumulative effect of creating divisiveness and destabilization. If predictions are accurate, in 50 years whites will no longer be the majority culture in the United States. Moreover, we may no longer be linked together by a common language and set of values. Our whole country may turn out to be like the occupants of an elevator heading to the top of the Empire State Building—a jamboree of different languages, accents, and customs. Embracing diversity is one thing, but what happens when it occurs at the expense of all of us working together for common goals? Are we really all that different from one another in terms of what we want out of life?

Regardless of our political affiliations, ethnic identification, or other cultural markers, most of us want basically the same things—a feeling of safety, that we are free from threat of harm; a sense of belonging among a group of peers who respect and value us; sufficient resources to meet basic needs and purchase things to improve the quality of our lives; opportunities to be productive and do something useful; and so on. These values are universal; they transcend cultures. Nevertheless, the focus of many of our discussions in the media, educational literature, and the teachers' lounge is on the differences between each of us and how much they complicate our lives.

Disorientation Facing Different Cultures

All our lives, we have been fascinated by what happens internally when the world is turned upside down. Just like the child who crumbles to the ground in helpless glee after spinning out of control, we have been both attracted and repulsed to opportunities as adults in which we could take ourselves to the brink of vertigo.

For a teacher walking into a classroom full of students for the first time, this is an experience that certainly qualifies as extremely disorienting. The sensation we experience as we scan the room trying to get a feeling for what is going on, identifying which children seem like trouble and which ones will be most responsive, is indeed a new cultural experience. Every classroom represents a unique blend of individual histories and customs, similar yet quite unlike any other we have seen before.

When we meet a new class, it feels like a first date, with all the accompanying apprehension, nervousness, and excitement. Will they like you? Will you like them? How will you get along? The main difference, of course, is that you are pretty much stuck with one another whether or not you share common interests and background.

The feeling of dizziness wears off in a little while—just about the time it takes to adjust to any strange new culture, whether you are traveling in a foreign country or visiting an ethnic restaurant. At first, you are struck by the strangeness and the differentness of the sights, sounds, and smells. Then you begin to make adjustments to what is going on around you. If you stay there long enough, what initially felt so weird will soon appear quite natural, sparking a different kind of disorientation—one that resembles the satisfaction and elation that comes from making a difference in other people's lives.

It is striking how different cultures are that have developed under similar circumstances. No doubt, you have noticed how classes, from year to year or even from period to period, can have such different personalities. Some are highly spirited; others seem lethargic. Year after year, you have attempted to provide the same stable set of norms for the kind of culture that you believe contributes most to constructive learning, but what actually develops is unpredictable.

Some classes evolve cooperatively, whereas others present continual tension. Sense of humor is a major part of one group—they are silly, spontaneous, and fun loving; another apparent clone of this group, however, seems grim and unresponsive.

We are puzzled by these differences in classroom atmosphere because our own internal culture seems so stable—our basic values and preferences, how we like to operate in our classes and lives, remain relatively constant. For example, I have noticed that, compared to a few other teacher friends, I enjoy a different level of classroom energy than they do. Not only can I tolerate a high degree of chaos around me but also, in some ways, I like a certain degree of conflict and dissonance as a way to keep things exciting. I feel disappointed in a class when they are too obedient and cooperative. I feel uncomfortable with the amount of effort devoted to win and maintain my approval.

Other teachers have quite different preferences in the classroom cultures they attempt to structure. They like an organized flow of activities, with each child focused on the task at hand. Distractions are held to a minimum; interruptions are not tolerated. Everyone is working together toward a common purpose. Everything is orchestrated carefully, with the period unfolding from a predetermined script.

Although I speak of these cultures within each teacher as relatively stable forces, the reality is somewhat more complex. In fact, depending on the particular situation we find ourselves in, the people with whom we are with, and even the mood we are in, we might embrace a number of different cultural values. This contributes to the collective disorientation we all feel when trying to predict one another's behavior when it changes according to whims, moods, setting, or even the weather.

Entrenched Positions and Changing Cultural Values

I was standing in the stairwell talking to an African American colleague about where we would go for lunch when two faculty members from another department approached us from the floor above.

"What is this, a drug deal?" one of them chided as she passed us.

My colleague responded to her with absolute seriousness: "Would you have said that if I wasn't a black man?"

She stopped in midstride, turned to face him, and clarified: "Actually I wasn't thinking about you as much as I was him [pointing to me] standing there in those old jeans and T-shirt, hands stuffed in his pockets as if he's hiding something." Then she giggled to herself, shook her head in puzzlement, and continued her descent.

I, too, thought my colleague had overreacted, and told him so: "Why must everything be about race, or about being African American?"

"Because we are the group that has been most discriminated against in this country," he replied more hotly than he intended.

I interrupted, "Oh yeah, what about the ways that Asian and Mexican immigrants are being treated in some parts of this country? What about Native Americans living in poverty on reservations that are every bit as hopeless as any inner-city ghetto? And they don't even have the fantasy of an athletic scholarship to entice them."

It was clear at this point, if not long before, that my friend and I were not exactly understanding one another. My arguments seemed so logical, so convincing, so . . . so right that I could not figure out why he could not hear me, much less alter his position. I believed he was being as ethnocentric and prejudiced as any stereotypic redneck. I was also quite aware that our continued dialogue on this subject was not leading us anywhere productive. We were both frustrated, both convinced the other was patently wrong in his point of view. Furthermore, there was not the slightest chance that anything either one of us was going to say would influence the other person's position.

Since that time, I have become increasingly aware of how often I hear people discussing issues related to culture, supposedly debating for the purposes of clarifying their own positions as well as influencing those of the other person, when it is quite apparent that there is not the slightest possibility that either party is going to change. The beliefs we hold about culture seem to be so ingrained, so impervious to challenge, that they are "givens" that define who we are.

Ironically, although our opinions about these issues are often resistant to change through direct dialogue, they are quite easily altered by the more subtle forms of enculturation controlled by the media, advertising industry, and political structures. Pass a law in which there is a tax incentive for putting money into a retirement account and all of a sudden the value of saving for the future becomes a more important cultural value. Pass another law in which certain entertainment expenses are no longer tax deductible and then the public loses its taste for expensive restaurants.

One blatant example of cultural engineering by a government has been initiated by the ruling party of Singapore, which receives considerable guidance from social scientists and public relations experts. In the 1980s, a campaign was set in motion to reduce the population growth of this tiny island nation by making it appear socially irresponsible to have more than one or two children. Not only was a media blitz launched on posters throughout the country but also a citizen's likelihood of getting a subsidized low-cost housing unit was directly related to compliance with this mandate of a single child. Within a few years, the government was able to reduce significantly the birth rate of its population merely through establishing new cultural norms. This media campaign was so successful, in fact, that the number of educated Chinese families (the dominant culture) was being overwhelmed by ethnic minorities, such as Malays and Indians, who were continuing to grow large families.

The same government that is so successful in controlling even public spitting and flushing toilets through fines decided to alter its policy, initiating a new campaign directed to Chinese families. New posters emerged throughout the subways showing happy, smiling families with two or more children. Sure enough, within a few years, the birth rates among Chinese climbed again.

Although we may be appalled at these "strong-arm" tactics to control social behavior, our own cultural norms are just as easily altered. Whether we are speaking of tastes in food, music, fashion, leisure pursuits, or what opinions are most attractive to hold, our views are easily changeable. For example, look at how propaganda has operated to alter the public opinions of our nation's leaders. Richard Nixon's image, which evolved from a promising feisty freedom fighter to an opportunist, an astute leader of foreign affairs, a betrayer of the Constitution, a discredited crook, a wise elder statesman, and then deification upon his death, demonstrates how easily our minds are changed. Incredibly, these changes in perception depended less on Nixon's behavior at a given time than on the slant taken by his handlers and the media. The goal of a press conference, lobbyist, media interview, or any other form of public relations is to put a particular spin on a desired point of view.

How our cultural values have changed can be demonstrated just as easily with regard to gender roles as with the historical legacy of a president. In a satire of these changes in our fickle cultural beliefs, Stein (1994) examined how quickly things have evolved for men who embrace the ideal norms of the time. Once upon a time, but a few decades ago, there was the "Insensitive Man." He was an avid capitalist and a guy who wore Old Spice, watched *Gunsmoke*, wore wide ties, drank beer, ate pepperoni pizza, and initiated sex aggressively.

Then there was the "Sensitive Man," embodied in the likes of Alan Alda of *MASH* fame and talk show host Phil Donahue. The Sensitive Man was a guy who drank light beer with his duck sausage pizza and quiche. He did not wear ties at all but buttoned his shirt to the top. Instead of cologne, he wore moisturizer. Rather than adopting the seductive posture of Tarzan, he found impotence to be fashionable.

Now, just a few years later, the cultural norms have changed once again, spawning the "Postsensitive Man." Timberland hiking boots, macaroni and cheese, and pumping iron—these are the symbols of this new guy. He eats meat loaf, wears his sweat proudly, and, with regard to his sexual habits, is comfortable reaching orgasm before his partner. He does not complain any more or express his feelings. He is a complicated guy: "Thoughtful and crude. Supportive and self-absorbed. And, in almost every circumstance, able somehow to think hard about two things at once. Like, say, a domestic-policy briefing and what's under the tight, pinstripe business suit of the woman delivering it" (Stein, 1994, p. 63).

The rules of cultural conduct, they are a'changin.' During the presensitive era of the 1950s, one's ethnicity, religion, and cultural origins were a matter of shame if you did not fit into the majority mold.

The sensitive era of the 1960s and 1970s was a time of burgeoning cultural pride—for example, black power, gay awareness, women's movement, men's movement, Hispanic coalition, and the Jewish Defense League.

Now, the postsensitive era of the 1990s and beyond is seeing affirmative action under the gun and the environment once again ripe for rape and pillage. Buffalo are no longer an endangered species; they are an exotic meal.

We must also consider changes that are happening in school classrooms in this postsensitive era. An emphasis on group focus is changing classroom curricula; federal funding is being funneled into schools that claim to be "at risk"; English as a Second Language programs have sprung up almost everywhere; academic tracking has become a mainstay; infusion is the new buzzword; non-native English speakers have emerged in even remote rural areas. This kind of group focus and obsession with labels is permanently changing school landscapes: The cultures of teachers, students, and schools have been transformed into political and cultural battlefields, with each culture vying for influence and control.

Cultures of Teachers, Students, and Schools

In examining cultural characteristics that distinguish people, as well as bring them together, we cannot help but be struck by differences evident in various student groups, teacher groups, and school cultures. In addition to how these three primary types of cultures impact educational practices, there are also influences from parents' cultures and those of the larger community of which schools are only one part.

School Culture

Ordinarily, we think of culture as it is applied to a person's ethnic background, racial or religious identification, or even socioeconomic class. If culture is broadly defined as socially transmitted norms that instill organized patterns of behavior in a particular group, then clearly there are distinct cultures operating in the classroom, as well as in the school itself. There is a "kid's culture," a "teacher's culture," and certainly several identified cultures in every school and each classroom within that building.

If we begin with a glimpse into a school's culture, we can find a unique atmosphere prevalent. These norms are established both intentionally by the principal and other administrators and implicitly by the behavioral codes evident in the students' and teachers' actions.

They are also influenced by a host of other factors—for example, the physical environment, community political realities, regional and neighborhood values, parental preferences, resources available, and historical legacies.

For example, I provide a look at two different high schools located in the same urban area. Both were built within a few years of one another. Both are approximately the same size and serve a constituency of children who are from roughly the same socio-economic background and parallel racial and ethnic representation. Each school, however, has a very different cultural climate.

Babe Ruth High School has received national attention because of its athletic programs. Its baseball teams have won the state championship 5 of the past 7 years. Its football teams and girls' softball teams are dominant in the district. They are quite proud of the fact that one of their swimmers has a shot at making the Olympic team. More than half of their golfers and tennis players received scholarships to Division I universities.

All these athletic accomplishments are proudly displayed as you first walk into the building and see the gleaming trophy case, crowded with honors and tribulations accrued over the years. Talk to the principal for any length of time and you will hear him recite the latest in a long series of athletic miracles that occurred at his school. This prowess on fields of play is definitely part of this school's culture. It trickles through almost every aspect of daily functioning—the announcements that are read over the public address system, how resources are allocated, the priority for how coaches are hired, and who has greatest status in the school among both teacher-coaches and student-athletes. This is a distinct culture, one that has many advantages and also some side effects.

By contrast, Bertrand Russell High School has not had its baseball, basketball, or football teams win more than half their games in more than a decade, although its women's field hockey team did advance to the state tournament the previous year (they lost in the first round). This is one of the elite academic public schools in the city. It had 12 national merit finalists last year. Graduates go to Stanford, Harvard, Massachusetts Institute of Technology, and even Oxford and the Sorbonne.

Located in the suburbs, Russell High has a culture that is highly regimented and achievement oriented. The competition is just as fierce as it is at Ruth High School but on quite a different playing field. Here, status is determined by class ranking, grade point average, and college aspirations. Obviously, a different school culture prevails, one with its own benefits and limitations. In this case, kids care more about grades rather than learning; teachers care more about order and discipline rather than creativity or fun.

I present these examples not as models to strive for but as contrasting cultures that influence what teachers and students do in these schools. Every occupant of these buildings feels pressure, in one way or another, to be a particular way. Teacher success is judged by different standards, just as student popularity is based on different priorities.

Classroom Culture

Although there may be a distinct and identifiable culture of a school, each classroom develops its own norms as well. We often marvel at this phenomenon. For example, a third-grade teacher does exactly the same things he or she has done the previous 7 years, but each class has its own personality. Even more remarkable, a high school teacher has three sections of world history but each group of students is as different as it could be. The history teacher follows the same lesson plans and initiates the identical activities in each section, but how each class of students interacts with him or her and the content he or she teaches is very different. For example, second hour is a rowdy group. It's like they're on speed. They laugh a lot, joke around with me, want to have a good time. Today I asked them to discuss in groups the main factors that contribute to civil wars in society. I couldn't shut them up! And their responses were so creative.

Fourth hour is from a different planet. They look at me placidly, waiting to see if I am really serious. They speak in whispers. Many of the students seem so tired, or maybe they're just hungry because lunch is next hour. Anyway, they have very low energy and offer very little in the way of enthusiasm or excitement.

Sixth hour is a different animal altogether. One thing they've got is energy but it is so *raw*. There's a lot of conflict in that group. They don't work well together. I have to rely on less interactive kinds of activities or they will end up at one another's throats.

Classroom culture results from a combination of many influences, just as it occurs in the larger school community. The teacher

Table 3.1 Cultural Forces in the Classroom: Teacher's Perspective

Organizational norms	Tribal coalitions
Administrative policy	Mutual goals
School culture	Physical or emotional attraction
Physical environment	Reciprocal altruism
Prescribed roles	Interpersonal bonding
Professional norms	**Perceived similarity**
Systemic Interaction	Reciprocal Influence
Clash or mesh of cultures	Control and power
Conflicts of interest	Modeling
Established patterns	Vicarious reinforcement
Emerging rituals	
Language	
Developmental evolution	**Interpersonal style**
Stages of trust	Ways of relating
Group dynamics	Empathy
Group roles	Cultural sensitivity
Individual or group development	Climate of trust
Projections	**Threats to safety or stability**
Distortions	Resistance
Prejudices	Denial
Transference	Overcompliance
Past experience	Risking

sets the tone, of course, based on his or her personality, teaching style, and goals. There is also an interactive effect, a kind of chemical soup, that results in unique outcomes depending on several ingredients, such as the composition of the class and what is going on in each person's life in that moment in time.

Student Culture

The following example is from the point of view of the high school student sitting in the back of the room:

The student feels like a piece of taffy being pulled from a hundred different directions at the same time. The teacher drones on about something or other that she thinks is so important. The student's mind is starting to drift. He catches a glimpse of thigh on the girl sitting next to him—a girl whose attention he has been trying to capture for some time without much success.

He is a little afraid of this teacher and a little in awe. Her opinion of him is important. She seems pretty smart, knows her stuff, and is fair. When she has been on his case about something, he usually deserved it. Therefore, he is doing his best to give her some significant part of his time and energy, but there is that girl.

He hears a cough to his right—one of his buddies trying to get his attention, snickering into his hand about something or other. He sees a note is heading his way and feels momentarily irritated. How is he supposed to concentrate on anything with all these distractions? This is really the least of his concerns. He knows what is waiting for him at home. Even if he wanted to do his homework after school, he has no private place to work. His mother will be nagging him to clean up the house and take care of his younger sisters. If his parents have been fighting, he can expect to be in the middle of another war. His friends will drop by to urge him to join them on some foray into enemy territory. Then there is that thigh that he can still see out of the corner of his eye.

Teacher Culture

If the previous example is how one student is being affected by various cultural influences operating in his life—in this case, to undermine his focus on education—it is interesting to consider how a teacher might look at the same culture in the classroom. Just as the student is feeling pulled in so many directions by various cultures in his life, so too is the teacher's behavior the result of competing forces, each vying for control (Table 3.1).

As the following example indicates, this teacher is subject to just as many cultural forces as any of her students.

She looks toward the back of the room and sees a young man, one of her favorites, casting his eyes to the girl on his right. She sees the note making its way to him from another direction. Sigh.

She feels a lot of pressure to do well, and even more than that, to be the perfect teacher. Even after years in the field, she still cannot come close to the ideals she had once set for herself. Approval rules her life: the good opinion of her students, of course, but also that of many others. She wants to be liked by the kids and respected as someone they can trust. She knows, however, that this creates some resentment among her colleagues and even one of the assistant principals, who feels she is not tough enough. The approval of her peers is certainly important but so is the validation she can never seem to get from her own parents.

As she looks out across this room, she is quite aware of all the cultural pulls that are taking place, both within herself and within every person in the room. She sees the coalitional groups and how they compete with one another. She wonders, almost aloud, how she can hope to interest these young people in what she is offering when they all seem so distracted by other things in their lives that are probably a heck of a lot more important to them. If the truth were told, she reluctantly admits, there are a few things going on in her own life at this moment that also feel more significant to her than what she is doing with these kids.

Teacher Subcultures

Few workers in our society are more important than teachers—they are the very heartbeat of our country. It is the work of teachers that shapes the minds, bodies, souls, and spirits of future generations; this is an enormous responsibility. In both direct and indirect ways, teachers also work with their students' homes, families, parents, communities, and siblings. They also have to deal with the grudges, anger, insecurities, hyperactivity, apathy, and lethargy that students carry with them to school. Many teachers interact with students who catch on to things quickly in the classroom but, at the same time and in the very same classroom of students, must figure out how to teach the same content to those who need a little more time to learn or who might learn best another way.

Few groups in the workplace, however, are more oppressed, more manipulated, more scorned, more scrutinized, more controlled, and more cursed at than classroom teachers. In today's society, teachers are more akin to political pawns than to pedagogues. Many have little choice on what and how to teach; they are subject to the curriculum whims of legislators, special interest groups, administrators, education service centers, state agencies, federal departments, and university faculty. Little wonder that burnout in the teaching profession is so high.

The idea of culture takes on a whole new meaning when applied to teachers because of all the complex variables that enter into this internal perspective. To even speak about teacher culture is meaningless because there are so many different variations of a theme.

Professional culture is composed of norms that have been established by leaders in the field. These include ethical codes for appropriate behavior as well as standards of excellence that most practitioners believe are important. Examples include the maintenance of lesson plans or following a policy of equity in which students of different races, genders, or abilities are given the same opportunities to learn and grow.

Your particular professional culture would also be influenced by your level of education and participation in various organizations. Those with advanced degrees, and who are active in local and national teacher associations, would be affected most by these experiences.

School culture is officially established by the principal in which a certain "tone" is set. This is done through written policy statements, staff meetings, supervisory and disciplinary practices, and even hiring procedures in which administrators are screening for a particular kind of staff contribution. School culture is also influenced, to a great extent, by contributions from the central district office that establishes consistent standards across schools, by parents, and certainly by students as well.

Depending on the principal's style of leadership, delegation of responsibilities, and degree of staff empowerment, teachers also play a big role in creating a school culture. Through their participation in sponsoring clubs, coaching athletic teams, interacting with the community, as well as creating a particular atmosphere in the school through their collective behavior, a particular school culture emerges.

Classroom culture is created by each teacher, in negotiation with the students in a particular group. This is the culture in which we have the greatest control. We have the power to create a particular atmosphere, value system, learning environment, and style of interaction depending on what we consider most important. Variations in classroom culture are most evident in terms of (a) which rules are developed and how they are enforced; (b) the kinds of interactions that take place and what they tend to emphasize; (c) how order is maintained; (d) which customs and traditions are infused into daily functioning; and (e) the kinds of interventions that are used to manage classroom behavior, facilitate learning, or move things along toward desired goals.

For example, you could imagine quite different classroom cultures in one setting in which the most consistently enforced rule is "No talking in class unless you are recognized to speak" versus another setting in which the primary rule is "Be respectful and polite in all interactions with others."

Personal culture refers to all the aspects of a teacher's disposition on any given day, or even at any moment in time. Every decision you make, every choice, whether deliberate or beyond your awareness, is influenced by your internal needs, whims, moods, and previous interactions. In one situation, you might be inclined to react one way, whereas in another, involving a different student and circumstance, some other aspect of your personal culture plays a more dominant role.

Multiple Cultures That Interact

In speaking about a teacher's culture, I am referring to the dynamic interplay of each aspect that makes up a part of who we are. Picture, for example, that part of your professional culture that has led you to be the role of expert. You are the "answer person," the one who, in the eyes of your students, seems to never be at a loss for words, nor explanations, for why things are the way they are. You have adopted this role as part of your personal culture as well; it is an important source of your self-confidence as you walk through life. It neutralizes some of the negative messages you heard about yourself growing up. It empowers you to feel reasonably smart and capable. Sure enough, this professional posture of expert in your field serves you well in your interactions with students. They respect you because you know things that they do not.

There are times, however, when you do not respond to particular students in certain situations as an expert. It is also part of your personal culture to be a caregiver. For example, a student approaches you hesitantly with something important on his or her mind. The student shyly asks for your advice about a family conflict that is troubling him or her. Rather than telling the student what to do (and you do have a strong opinion about what would be best), you restrain your directive impulses and instead listen carefully and attentively, after which you offer him or her support and empathy:

> I really appreciate your trusting me enough to talk to me about this. I'm not sure what you should do either but I have confidence in you that you will figure out what is best. I want you to know how much I respect your good judgment and your ability to make sound decisions. So whatever you decide to do, or however you decide to handle this, I want you to know that I will support you. I may not do things exactly the way you might do them, and I may not even agree with the choices that you make, but I have faith in you as a person that eventually you will work things out. I guess what I am saying is that I really care about you.

Implicit in this message is a very different kind of personal culture other than teacher as expert. If anything, the teacher downplays himself or herself as an expert, instead relying on his or her role as a nurturing and supporting figure in this student's life. The teacher might not react the same way to all of his or her students. Much depends on the kind of relationship the teacher has developed with each of the students and also what is going on inside of him or her at any moment in time. Another important dimension is influenced by how teachers define themselves as professionals—in other words, what they see as their primary mission.

Teachers contend with professional, school, and classroom cultures, and these are blended together with their own personal culture. It is this personal culture—a very real culture composed of biographical, cultural, ethnic, religious, and family qualities—that determines teachers' classroom dispositions. In the midst of contending with all these forces, teachers also have personal culture that bears heavily on their teaching.

Confronting Biases and Prejudices

What is a teacher to do in a school and classroom culture in which the children appear to have so little in common or in which they literally do not speak the same language? We live in a country that is made up of 300 different ethnic groups. Even among supposedly unified groups, there are more differences among various subgroups than similarities. Native Americans are composed of 200 distinct tribes, and that does not even count the various bands of each tribe, many of which speak separate languages. Hispanics, a coalition of political convenience, include members of dozens of Latin American countries, each with its own unique set of customs, values, and dialects.

It is inevitable that a teacher, much less any of the students, would have distinct preferences toward some cultures rather than others, especially those that most resemble the teacher's own heritage. Usually, biases, prejudices, discrimination, and racism are viewed as a lack of experience, understanding, appreciation, or moral maturity on the part of individuals who develop negative attitudes toward others of a different background (Timm, 1996). Actually, such racial beliefs can be highly functional as a way to inflate the sense of superiority of one's own kind, protect employment opportunities for those who share one's values, redistribute resources in such a way that one's kind will benefit more than others, and identify scapegoats to blame when things are not going as well as one would like.

It is hardly fashionable, much less remotely acceptable, to admit that any of us holds prejudicial, discriminatory, or racist attitudes. We all walk around pretending as if we are free of such primitive beliefs. In fact, to be called "racist" is the kiss of death in most schools—a brand akin to being labeled a Nazi. To admit publicly being biased toward or against members of a particular group would likely result in social ostracism, if not sanctions or even dismissal from your job.

Within the privacy of our own minds, if not among our families and most trusted friends in the teachers' lounge, each of us harbors both racist and culturally biased attitudes. Because we are not allowed to admit these negative feelings, much less talk about them in an open forum, they remain underground and unchallenged. We go about our business refusing to acknowledge, much less confront, the stereotypical images we have of people who belong to other cultural groups. Those who claim to be most enlightened are adamant that they are exempt from such labels. In some ways, such teachers are almost as dangerous as publicly espoused racists because, without acknowledging subtle and unintentional biases, little can be done to change them.

Indeed, most of the time it is possible to maintain a degree of equanimity toward all people, regardless of color and customs. During difficult times, however, we temporarily suspend those attitudes that were convenient to hold when we could afford to be gracious. For example, when someone cuts you off on the freeway and then flips you an obscene gesture, this person is not only an individual but also a representative of a cultural group.

One other sensitive area is assuming that only white males, or those of the dominant culture, are capable of racism, sexism, or prejudice. Discrimination is widespread among all ethnic and cultural groups. Muslims believe they are better than Christians. Protestants think less of Catholics. Seventh-Day Adventists feel sorry for Jews, who in turn believe they are the "chosen people." Mormons are convinced they are more enlightened than others. Each religious group believes it has found the perfect path to spiritual enlightenment, whereas others have been led astray. This is no less true in the attitudes that Finns feel toward Norwegians, Greeks feel toward Turks, New Zealanders feel toward Australians, Cuban Americans feel toward Puerto Ricans, WASPs feel toward Irish Catholics, or Chicago Cubs fans feel toward supporters of the Chicago White Sox. It is among the most natural of human urges since the beginning of time to be suspicious of those not like us and to disparage their differences in customs and habits.

It is interesting, even unnerving, to consider your own biases and prejudices toward members of particular groups. How willing would you be, for example, to marry, or have your child marry, someone of the following cultures:

Seventh-generation English	Muslim
Jew	Filipino
Cuban American	Mexican American
Chinese American	Kenyan
Amish	Jehovah's Witness
American Indian	Haitian

The following are a few more questions to consider:

- Among your friends and closest confidantes, how many are members of cultures, races, and religions different from your own?
- Two children in your class are involved in a disagreement. One of them is a member of your race and culture, and the other is not. What do you feel inside as you view the behavior of each child?
- You see a mixed-race couple kissing on the street. What is your gut-level reaction?
- How many times in the past month have you socialized with someone of a different race?
- Which ethnic group consistently does best in your classes and which does worst? Assume that this difference in performance is related not only to student characteristics but also to teacher behavior. How might you be treating students of one culture differently than others?
- How are you aware that you treat boys differently from girls in your classroom?

How you would answer these questions depends not only on your experiences and sensitivity to people of different backgrounds but also on your own internal culture. As I mentioned previously, each of us has a particular cultural identity that is blended from ethnic, religious, socioeconomic, gender, racial, familial, and other influences. The filters through which we see others have been shaped according to training in the past. In part, some of us have been trained to be exploiters and others to be their victims.

In Chapter 4, the nature of biases, prejudices, and cultures that lead to misunderstandings and conflict is explored in greater depth. Ignorance is not an excuse for neglect, or inflicting harm on others, just because we are not aware of our distinct preferences.

Some Cultural Misunderstandings

An amazing degree of flexibility and adaptability is required on the part of a teacher to continuously make adjustments in thinking and action in light of new awareness about the various cultures within and between students. Misunderstandings most often take place when one or both parties insist on a course of action without incorporating feedback that is continuously being provided.

It Always Worked Before

We were all a little nervous as class began, each of us trying to make a good impression. I was a visitor in their country, a guest instructor in an education course designed to look at different approaches to promoting change. I would be with them for the next several weeks, charged with introducing them to some North American perspectives that might be incorporated into their New Zealand classrooms.

The first thing I did was put them into a circle and direct them to introduce themselves to one another and to me. The idea was for each of the 20 students to spend approximately 3 minutes briefly telling us something about who they are. I am sure this is an activity that is familiar to most of us in similar circumstances.

Indeed, things seemed to develop just as I imagined they would. Although most of the introductions were fairly superficial, even after modeling as much openness and honesty as I could muster in a few minutes, the procedure spread rapidly around the circle, each person taking the allotted time to tell us something about his or her background or goals—that is, until one darker skinned young man took his turn. Characteristic of his people, he first launched into the traditional Maori greeting, telling me about the origins of the area in which his family had lived for generations. I gently instructed to him to speak to everyone in the group, not just to me, but his eyes never wavered from mine.

Five, 10, 15 minutes had gone by and he was still talking, telling us about the mountain and river that he identified with and the family he was part of but still not saying anything about who he was as an individual. To further complicate matters, much of what he was saying was in the Maori language, a tongue about which I knew next to nothing.

I could see the others in the class were growing uneasy, even some of the other Maori students. I glanced at my watch and realized we would never finish this task unless we moved along fairly quickly. Back in the States, I would have not thought twice about abruptly stepping in and urging the young man to be more concise, or perhaps even telling him that his time was up and we had to move on. I was unsure, however, what the conventions and customs were in New Zealand culture. I desperately wanted to make a good impression, and I did not know if I would offend more people by intervening or not intervening.

I wondered at the time if I was being overly indulgent; after all, if this had been one of the other students, I would have jumped in almost immediately to redirect the focus. Would I have allowed someone of Irish heritage to go on for 20 minutes about his or her lineage when the assignment was to briefly say something about who you are? Of course not. Maybe the rules are a bit different in this country about what is considered appropriate, however.

A few more minutes elapsed while I was going over in my head what I should do. Finally, I could stand it no longer and so said in my most gentle voice, "I really appreciate how much you are sharing but we really have to move on to others. I wonder if you might summarize a few of the most important things you would like us to know about you."

It was as if I had slapped him. Immediately, his eyes went down and he mumbled something I could not quite make out. I looked around the room and saw that others were extremely uncomfortable by what had just transpired. Were they embarrassed for him, though, or for me?

The young man visibly withdrew from the class. He even scooted his desk a few feet outside of the circle, as if he was no longer part of this group. I could hear the buzz of whispers all around me, each person offering his or her own opinion to one another about what took place. It was clear that some major transgression had taken place—one that I had been part of.

I quickly apologized. Apparently, I had done something offensive by interrupting him before he was finished. I tried to explain that I had only been concerned about the time and that I wanted to make sure that everyone had a chance to present themselves. If I had let him go on, it would have been at the expense of others who would be left out.

As reasonable as this explanation sounded to my ears (and perhaps to yours as well), I now had made matters worse. I had not only censured him in front of his peers but also humiliated him further by communicating that I was disappointed in his behavior. I could see his cheeks flush and feel his anger at being misunderstood. Even worse, I could see how this resentment toward my insensitivity was now spreading around the room.

This student was not the only person who had been misunderstood! Now I was feeling upset as well! Jeez, I was only trying to be helpful. Can't they give me a break? How am I supposed to know what the rules are? Why all this attention just because he is a Maori student? This would never have happened with anyone else.

I decided it was time for a break. Just as the student escaped from the room, I rushed to intercept him in the hallway. I reiterated my regret that I had done something to offend him. I asked his indulgence of my ignorance about his culture. I was new in his country and did not know the appropriate ways of acting. As I continued on with my pleadings, he never raised his eyes once, never responded except to nod his head. He never returned to class again.

In retrospect, it is easy for me to let myself off the hook. Perhaps this was not a cultural misunderstanding at all but rather inappropriate conduct on the part of one individual student who just happened to be of the indigenous people of his island. After all, there were several other Maori students who followed the instructions, and there were many other cultures represented that also deserved fair attention. Also, I did not mean to hurt him or anyone else. It should have been evident to him, and everyone else, that I was only trying to do my job.

Why, then, am I still haunted by this episode of cultural misunderstanding? If it is so clear that this incident was an anomaly, an unavoidable conflict with an unreasonable student, then why am I so convinced that I bear some responsibility for the problem?

I consulted with a dozen different people after this class, trying to understand what happened and why. I spoke with students in the class and several trusted New Zealand colleagues. Although I expected to have my perspective validated, even to receive some sympathy at how I had been treated, what I got instead only heightened my unease.

The problem was the structure that I introduced in the first place. In the past, it had been a foolproof way for me to begin a class—a strategy I have tried a hundred times before in a dozen other places. I was unwise, however, to expect that a similar outcome would take place with a very different population, no matter how similar the context may appear.

Several people proceeded to tell me what they would have done differently if they had been starting the class with such an activity— ideas that never would have occurred to me. I was also amazed to learn about the alternative ways there would have been to handle the critical incident after it had occurred. For example, far better than to have brought even more attention publicly to the incident, I should have approached an intermediary to speak to the student on my behalf. Also, I should have let the student finish no matter how much time it would take. One question I was asked again and again was why it was so important that I finish the activity in the allotted time. Was there something more important than allowing students to present themselves with dignity?

Neglect or Overreaction?

Sometimes attention to cultural sensitivity can be taken to an extreme, to the point where almost everything you do or say must first be run through an internal multicultural censor to make sure you will not offend someone. Someday there may come a point when we all stand before our classes mute, absolutely paralyzed with the realization that almost anything that comes out of our mouths may upset somebody.

For example, a woman of Cherokee Indian heritage made a point of striking up a conversation with me during the break of a workshop I was doing on relationships. We bantered a bit before she finally disclosed how much she was enjoying the day's activities. When I later looked back out at the audience, it felt good to see her face among the crowd.

After another segment, she was one of the few who felt comfortable asking a question—one about why I thought Indian relationships still retained a number of rituals during healing encounters, whereas our contemporary culture did not include them as part of counseling or teaching. Facetiously, I remarked, "I guess because we're civilized." Picking up the cue, she replied, "Right. And we're primitive." It felt good that she had gotten the point, and I could feel the connection between us. I also liked how I had been able to emphasize the contrast between cultures for the audience—or so I believed.

When I read the evaluations of the day, one participant remarked that, although previously she had greatly admired my work, she now realized I was something of a fraud. She cited as evidence the example of my incredible insensitivity to call an Indian primitive, in public even!

I was aghast at her interpretation of my comment. Must I be so careful in the future that I cannot joke about an idea to drive home its point? How interesting that her perception of the exchange led her to conclude I was callous when, in fact, I was exhibiting what I believed to be a special connection to a person's culture. It is very easy for actions to be misunderstood or blown out of proportion to their intent.

One example of this phenomenon occurred in a middle school in a small town in California. A 14-year-old Indian child was found to be carrying a pouch with a suspicious-looking substance in it, at the very least composed of tobacco and perhaps even a more illicit drug. The school has a policy of zero tolerance for tobacco or any drug. The student explained that the pouch had religious significance to her, and that it was given to her by her father to protect her from bad influences. School administrators decided to investigate further, so they cut open the pouch to examine its contents, which, on analysis, were found to be a mixture of tobacco and sage. Consistent with school policy, she was sent home.

Tribal leaders in the area were incensed that she was punished for merely following her cultural heritage. School administrators' attempts to apologize for this misunderstanding did little to mollify what was perceived as assaults to their dignity. A relatively simple mistake quickly escalated into a major conflict based not so much on current circumstances as on historical legacies.

I wonder how many others I have lost over the years through such mistakes? So tricky is this subject of culture that it seems that a single misstep, or even misinterpretation, can damn a spirit of trust and respect. Another comment that was noted on my evaluation form was the acknowledgment that "Perhaps I have a need to see you as perfect. Once you said what you did, I realized you say stupid things just like me. Rather than feeling good about this, I felt sad." Oh, the need to maintain illusions among our mentors!

I have heard repeatedly by members of ethics boards and malpractice attorneys that the professionals most likely to be sued by their clients are those who are cold, aloof, arrogant, or nonresponsive. Therapists and doctors who make an effort to be nice to people are more often given the benefit of the doubt or even forgiven for making mistakes. The same is true for teachers as well.

Very often, children perceive those of us who are doing our very best to help them as meddlesome at best and often an enemy who is attempting to make their lives miserable. Sometimes even the most genuine effort to offer support can easily be misinterpreted as something quite different. In Freedman's (1995) novel about a 14-year-old boy struggling as a member of the underclass culture, the main character explains why he has given up at school. A teacher speaks to him after an altercation:

> "You're smart boys, there's no reason you shouldn't be doing better."
> We nodded our heads and shuffled our feet. We get this all the time from teachers, how we're really smart and just don't apply ourselves. I've been hearing that shit from first grade. Actually, it's true. At least I am, I don't know about other guys, but I can be smart when I want to be. The only

thing is, who cares about being smart in such a dumb school? The other thing is I don't look like a brain or act like one so my teachers treat me like I'm dogshit, which is how they treat most of the kids here. It's not exactly the best way to get somebody to do better.

In any difference of opinion, there are always two sides. From a teacher's perspective, this child appears to be a major trouble-maker—surly, uncooperative, and completely unmotivated. Each party finds fault with the other, blaming him or her for the mis-understanding.

A student chorus would sing, "If only teachers could understand what we are going through, they wouldn't treat us this way."

Teachers would respond, "If only kids would realize we are only trying to help them."

Your Role in the Conflict

Cultural misunderstandings, or any relationship conflict, result from one or both parties being unwilling or unable to grasp the context for the other's experience. It is a time-honored tradition at the university that graduate students are often put through the gauntlet of academic rigor in which they are required to write a thesis and then "defend" their paper against an onslaught of faculty members who test for intellectual mettle to see if this candidate has the right stuff before he or she is allowed to graduate. During one such exercise, I served as the outside representative on a thesis committee in political science. The student, an ex-diplomat from an Asian country, was presenting his thesis on a contemporary political issue. He was an older gentleman, quite distinguished and obviously worldly. He sat stiffly in his chair, obviously and understandably nervous as he faced this formidable group of professors who were scrutinizing him carefully to see if he belonged in the exclusive club.

The chairperson began the meeting on a friendly note, asking the student if he was nervous, to which he immediately shook his head no. That is strange, I thought, he sure looks anxious to me. The chairperson then proceeded to tell a story of how he remembered being in a similar circumstance many years previously and how he had been so apprehensive that his voice came out as a squeak. The student smiled tightly, looking straight ahead.

Things did not go well for the student this day. What appeared initially to be anticipatory tension blossomed full blown into incapacitating anxiety. He did not seem to hear the questions that were directed his way. His answers were long and rambling, often unrelated to what had been asked. He appeared disoriented, confused, and lost. It was a puzzling situation. He was a career diplomat, obviously highly experienced in his field, and also an able student who had distinguished himself in his academic courses, but he failed miserably at the task of discussing a piece of work that he knew so well that he had virtually had it memorized. What, on earth, had happened?

As I replayed the scenario in my mind, I recalled the initial question that had been intended to set him at ease. How inappropriate, it occurred to me, to ask an Asian diplomat if he was nervous. What a loss of face that would imply if he were to admit to such a weakness! As I began to get a glimpse of the extent of our cultural misunderstanding, I realized the extent to which he had been subjected to ritual humiliation. No wonder he could not concentrate!

That could not possibly excuse his dismal performance, however. I had argued in the private meeting after he left the room that perhaps he was not ready to graduate. After all, he could not even respond to simple questions about a subject in which he was supposed to be an expert. My colleagues agreed with my assessment but, to my surprise, did not seem nearly as upset with how things had gone. Unwilling to rock the boat, I went along with their decision to pass him, assuming they must have different academic standards on this part of campus. Only afterward was it explained to me that the student had a hearing impairment. The reason he could not respond intelligently to some of the questions was that, because of the positioning of seats around the table, he could not see some of us well enough to read our lips.

I think about this example of teacher-student misunderstanding quite often when I am aware of some conflict with a student. Although my first inclination is to assume that this person is just being difficult, ungrateful, lazy, or manipulative, I force myself to consider the context for his or her behavior. I ask myself several questions internally to sort out this relationship impasse (Kottler, Sexton, & Whiston, 1994) (Table 4.1).

Table 4.1 Internal Questions

Professional Assessment	Personal Reaction
What are the ways that this relationship is not working?	How am I overreacting to what is taking place?
What is the cultural context for the child's experience?	What am I expecting from this person?
How might I alter my working diagnosis?	How have I distorted the picture?
What interventions have been most and least helpful?	What am I doing to drive the child away?
What is the child doing that is getting in the way?	How has my humanness been withheld or diluted?
Who has an interest in sabotaging the relationship?	How am I making things worse?
How is the child avoiding issues through resistance?	What am I avoiding or unwilling to explore?
What outside resources can I access (colleagues, research)?	How can I learn from this encounter?

These internal questions imply a different kind of strategy altogether than the one that usually takes place in a teacher's head or later in the teachers' lounge when we recruit sympathy and support for our positions. Our first inclination is often to place blame onto the offending students, as if they are the problem and if only they would act in accordance with our expectations there would not be a problem (readers are nodding their heads enthusiastically: "You have missed the boat on a number of issues but at least you got that one right!"). What these questions force us to do, however, is look at many conflicts between teachers and students as essentially cultural misunderstandings in which we have shared responsibility for what has gone wrong.

This assumption leads to very different strategies for resolving problems with so-called difficult students. Because all conflicts are the result of an interactive effect in which both parties are responsible for the misunderstanding, it is senseless to assign blame. Efforts should instead be devoted as much to figuring out what we are doing to create or exacerbate the problem as to the student's perceived disruptive behavior (J. Kottler, 1994). This could involve any of the following predicaments in which the teacher is actually the one who is igniting the conflict, if not making it much worse than it needs to be (Kottler, 1992, 1997a):

- *The teacher is expecting things the student is unable to do.* For example, you ask a child to come to the board to do a demonstration problem. He persistently refuses. It is not so much that he does not want to cooperate, however, as it is that he is unable to do so because he never had the requisite preparation that would have allowed him to understand what you are asking him to do.
- *The teacher is expecting things the student is unwilling to do.* Sometimes, requests of students are made that seem perfectly reasonable to us but are actually quite unacceptable to others. For example, it certainly seems appropriate to ask students to share something they are proud of, unless it goes against their cultural upbringing to "brag" about themselves.
- *The teacher is missing information that is critical to understanding the context for the behavior.* For example, you reach out to touch a second grader reassuringly, but she recoils and pushes you away. You think to yourself that this student is obstructive and resistant—until you later find out that she has been sexually abused by other adults she had once trusted.
- *The teacher is subscribing to invalid assumptions.* There are times when you believe you know things that you really do not. An example of this is the story at the beginning of the chapter in which I assumed the Asian diplomat was a poor student, when actually his poor performance had been initially triggered by a major cultural gaffe that had then been exacerbated by a physical disability.

- *The teacher is engaging in some activity, technique, or intervention so ineptly and insensitively that he or she is creating the resistance.* For example, your intention is to quiet a student who is a little too boisterous. You censure the student far more brutally than you realize. Thereafter, he or she shuts down, refusing to participate in future activities.
- *The teacher has lost compassion.* This is the most serious breach of all, one in which the teacher looks at students as the enemy and blames them for all troubles in the classroom. The teacher is convinced that it is the students' poor motivation, their poor preparation, or their parents' lack of concern that is creating conflicts. One aspect teachers forget to consider is what inside them is getting in the way of being more caring and compassionate toward the people they are paid to help.

I am used to receiving much resistance to these ideas when I present them at programs titled "Working With Difficult Students." Both therapists and teachers would much rather complain and place blame on those ungrateful, unmotivated, disruptive kids that ruin professional lives because they will not get with the program. I certainly do not mean to imply that there are not any kids out there who are genuinely difficult people to get along with—for anyone. I simply remind you that we bear some responsibility, as well, for any conflict in our lives—whether that is in our classrooms or at home with our own children, parents, spouses, or roommates. It has been shown, and will now be examined more closely, how disagreements often result not only from competing agendas (we want to get through our lesson plans, but our students want to have fun) but also from a clash of cultures that stress different values.

A Clash of Cultures

The cultures of the teacher, and those of the students, are rarely compatible; there are certainly different agendas at stake. Furthermore, the cultural values of mainstream education are not exactly responsive to the innumerable variations of culture that are represented in any group of children. For any institution to function, someone has to set some universal boundaries and rules for all to follow; unfortunately, these social conventions fit some people's background more than others. I briefly review several of the most predominant values of mainstream education and supply examples of how they are at odds with the customs of particular cultural groups we may see represented in our classrooms.

Being on Time

I have previously mentioned how the concept of time, and especially how it is perceived, varies from culture to culture. Even the definition of what it means to be "on time" is hardly a constant. For certain appointments in military or diplomatic circles, being on time means arriving at least 20 minutes before the scheduled session. Within North America and many non-Mediterranean European nations, time is also viewed within fairly rigid parameters. This is not the case, however, with many cultural groups on our continent.

Our schools are run on buzzers and bells, signaling precise transitions from one activity or class to the next. Enter a room 1 minute past the designated signal and you are tardy; worse than that, you are considered a discipline problem, an unmotivated student, and an irresponsible human being.

Within Hispanic cultures, however, time has quite a different meaning. Students might not be considered as "late" if they came within 10 or even 20 minutes of the target hour. There is a different value placed on the present over the future. Whatever you are doing right now is far more important than what you might get around to doing next. If you are involved in a meaningful activity, or engaged in an interesting discussion, it makes no sense to break it off just to be somewhere else. The culture of *mañana* means let tomorrow or the next hour wait; live for this moment.

Many Hispanic students come from homes in which time is not rigidly partitioned, enforced, or managed in the same ways that we may do so in our schools. "Be with you in a minute" does not mean the same thing to a Mexican American that it does to a German American. To the North American, "I'll be there around 2:00" means "I will be there at 2:00 precisely, or perhaps a few minutes before"; that same pronouncement by a Latin American means "I will be there some time mid-afternoon, depending on what else comes up."

Our students are thus not on an equal playing field when we expect them all to be capable and willing to comply with structures that we believe are quite reasonable and even necessary for schools to function. It is not that Hispanic students should be excused from the same time constraints as those that Asian and North American students comply with; we must keep in mind that other cultures do not necessarily think that being on time is all that important in the first place. In some ways, it gets in the way of learning.

It is absurd, in a way, that students heavily involved in a particular learning activity must abruptly stop to do something else that is scheduled next. I certainly do not claim to have an alternative structure in mind, at least one that is practical in today's schools. I do find it useful, however, to remember that some of the values of our educational system are designed not to facilitate learning but rather expediency.

Assertiveness

Taking individual initiative may be the mark of success in American culture, but it is certainly not part of the cultures to which many Asian children belong. In comparing the kinds of relationships that develop between students and teachers in the schools of both the United States and India, it is apparent that quite a number of differences emerge (see Kottler et al., 1994; Neki, 1976). Whereas we idealize the values of independence, autonomy, individuation, and assertiveness, Indian culture emphasizes teaching relationships in which the student is subservient, deferential, dependent, and approval seeking. It is not surprising, therefore, that children of Asian or Native American cultures would appear to be unduly passive, withdrawn, and disengaged to American teachers.

Logic

In our culture and schools, we stress the merits of logic over intuition, thinking over feeling, and deductive reasoning over supernatural forces. In many non-Western cultures, however, quite the opposite is stressed in their value systems. Interpretations and explanations for natural phenomena are less important than the rituals used to honor them. The forces of nature are considered to be far more powerful than the simple logic of human beings. Spiritual aspects of life are given far more credence and attention. Contemplation is stressed over analysis, which diminishes the essence of a thing.

In a sense, we are asking children from non-Western cultures to abandon the values that they were brought up with to fit into our world. This is not an unreasonable, or even an unusual, expectation. If you were attending school in India, Japan, or Borneo, you would be expected to fit into their educational value system as well. It sure helps in the adjustment process, however, if we understand the special challenges that are involved for children who are trying to reconcile discrepancies between what adults demand of them in school versus what is expected at home.

Written Language

Our schools often emphasize written discourse over spoken language, especially in most assignments. This agenda is considerably at odds with those cultures that have an oral tradition of language. Among people of Appalachia, Polynesia, or Native American tribes, for example, learning takes place through stories that are passed on from adults to children. Written language is not part of their heritage in the same way that songs, chants, folk tales, and stories are used. We expect these children, however, to abandon that which has been part of their homes for generations to use a different language system that is mostly unfamiliar.

The same can be said for spoken language as well. African American, Cuban American, or Puerto Rican dialects of English are spoken at home, with peers, and in local neighborhoods. These languages have their own vocabularies, accents, and traditions. They may not be valued within mainstream culture; the consequences of speaking "proper" English in the neighborhood, however, would be catastrophic for a child. He or she would be ridiculed mercilessly for selling out. It is fascinating indeed when we hear some of our students address us in carefully modulated, perfectly accented phrases, and then hear them speak to a peer.

You might ask, "Isn't this kind of obvious. Don't we already know that children speak different languages at home and in their neighborhoods than they do in the classroom?" Of course we know this, but we do not often remember the conflicts our students are struggling with when we ask them to do things that we think are important but are actually fairly low on their list of priorities.

Goal Oriented

Teacher preparation programs and school districts are in love with the notion of educational objectives. Whole courses, as well as chapters in most texts, are devoted to the subject. Generations of teachers have been forced to learn Benjamin Bloom's taxonomies of educational objectives, Robert Mager's use of specific instructional objectives, and Norman Gronlund's use of general objectives. It is as if the single best predictor of teaching excellence is the quality of lesson plans. It seems that unless we state specifically what we intend to teach, how we will teach it, and how we will assess the extent to which objectives are met, "real" learning cannot take place.

Although I certainly endorse the importance of strategic planning, and even the value of specifying and measuring outcomes, I also recognize that so much of learning takes place as a result of serendipitous circumstances in which the planned agenda was abandoned in favor of critical moments of opportunity. This, after all, is how learning naturally takes place in many cultures. The time to teach is when the child recognizes there is a need to learn.

The previous examples are just a few of the mainstream concepts that make learning difficult for children from different cultures. Most of these you have probably heard before in a text you once read or in a lecture you sat through. The greatest problem we have is not in realizing how easy it is to leave some children behind but rather in what we can possibly do to reach more of them.

Cultural misunderstandings exist because we do not take the time, or make sufficient effort, to learn about the context for behavior that we find perplexing or irritating. Of course, exactly the same can be said for students who misjudge our best efforts to help them. Very often, we feel frustrated because children respond to us as if we are an enemy who has been placed in this world to make their lives miserable.

All of us are just doing the best we can—the best we know how to do. We may readily agree that these efforts are not nearly good enough. One of the greatest contributions of expanding our multicultural awareness is that we are able to better appreciate the beauty and grace of cultural rituals and practices that are different from our own.

Beauty and Grace in School Rituals

Richard Powell
and
Jeffrey A. Kottler

School begins not with a bang or a whimper but with a bell. Children dutifully file through the door but not without a few last-minute interactions. They give one another handshakes so complex it looks like their wrists are dancing. A few children fortify themselves by unwrapping pieces of gum and carefully placing them in the hidden recesses of their mouths. Other children huddle in a circle around the side of the building, stomping out the last of their cigarette butts. One set of rituals ends while another one begins with the signal of the first bell.

The school has been designed to homogenize the children and to make them walk through the day as a disciplined army, one that can be managed with a minimum of fuss given their unbridled energy.

They will say the Pledge of Allegiance to start the day—a ritual designed to remind them that they are all in this together. Nobody is really paying attention, of course: They are trading food behind their backs, passing notes, and making eye contact as their way of reconnecting after a night apart.

Linking the idea of rituals to school life may not be very easy. Visions of chanting, swooning dancers, their bodies pulsating to the pounding of drums; this is an image that seems more familiar. Maybe you have an easier time relating rituals to religious ceremonies and practices such as communion, passing of the sacrament, baptism, lighting candles on the Sabbath, or reciting prayers. Who among us has not thrown rice on a newly joined couple as they leave for their ceremonial honeymoon—a rite of passage that symbolizes opening the doorway to sharing a portion of life together as partners?

Rituals help organize our lives in familiar patterns. They become signals for us to adopt particular frames of mind, social demeanors, or emotional tones. Shaking hands signals a form of ritual greeting. Kissing under a mistletoe, saying a blessing before a meal, and singing the national anthem before a sporting event are all common examples of these behavioral patterns that have been prescribed by social convention.

To think of students in school passing from one class to another as part of an elaborate ritual and to think of school administrators as being the keepers of ritual, however, seems odd. That is exactly what school life is all about, however—a ritualized way of existing day in and day out, with many different rites of passage all going on at the same time. Some of these rites of passage, however, are very narrow in scope, very demanding, certainly exclusionary, and have definite rules. Unfortunately, these same rites of passage in school classrooms do their best to squeeze the cultural life out of some students and to socialize students into ways of acting, knowing, and thinking that may very well be the exact opposite of what their home, family, and community are all about.

In this chapter, we explore the idea of schools as ritualized institutions. We consider what this kind of ritualized life means for the many different cultures in contemporary society that meet and mingle together. Also, we consider how pluralism, as a social and cultural reality, is challenging the kind of ritualized school life that has been maintained for many years by mainstream society. Most important, we consider how the beauty and grace of some students' ritualized lives have potential to broaden and deepen the social and academic interactions in classrooms, if only teachers would allow this to happen.

Structure of Rituals

Rituals are not just simple acts that join people together for superficial reasons. Rather, they are complex sets of behaviors that connect people together both explicitly and implicitly. Many rituals, especially those related to education and religion, have important histories; in fact, the origins of some practices are lost to those of us who are mandated to enforce them. It seems absurd to consider that the reason why high schools begin so early in the morning is so that students can be out early enough to work on their families' farms.

In American culture, most of the beauty and grace of our rituals seem to now be limited to sporting fields. Sport has taken on an almost religious fervor, a metaphor that goes deeper than we might think. Nixon and Frey (1996) list a number of comparisons between the two human activities, each of which has similar rituals that are recognizable not only in our school athletic teams but also everywhere else in our culture. In both sport and religion, there is a quest for perfection; an emphasis on self-discipline and denial; an integration of mind, body, and spirit; deep devotion and commitment; a special language; pilgrimages to shrines; claims of special virtue; worship of heroes; social control; and elements of magic. Even more striking for our subject are the established rituals and celebrations that are part of school sports, whether they involve chants, cheerleading, prescribed plays, or even special prayers offered by players and fans alike to recruit God to their side.

Except for sporting activities, rituals in our lives have become rather empty routines of going through the motions. They are often seen as rather thoughtless acts that look downright silly if you thought about them—kind of like crossing yourself or knocking on wood to prevent bad luck. Consequently, many rituals tend to be undervalued by our culture and are often not taken seriously.

Interestingly, the idea of daily routine, which is a phrase that we all fit ourselves into, is synonymous with ritualized life. Indeed, routines are representations of participants' lives (Lesko, 1988). Therefore, examining how we live together, within a particular context such as schools, and examining the historical aspects of the context can provide much insight into how ritualized lives provide structure for thinking, for acting, and for treating other people.

School life is quite literally saturated with rituals; some of them are just part of growing up, whereas others are more elaborate and appear harmless, such as crowning the queen at the homecoming football game. Still other rituals are more culturally challenging—for example, adhering to a set of linguistic codes suggested by the mainstream culture such as allowing only English to be spoken inside the school doors. Regardless of whether the rituals of school appear harmless or whether they are more culturally demanding, every student's life at school is structured, governed, and ruled by rituals.

Then and Now

In times past, teachers may have been successful with one style of teaching. Direct instruction, for example, was fashionable for a very long time and is still among the most popular forms of pedagogy. One of the reasons for its longevity is the perception that lecturing and testing is consistent with our cultural pride of efficiency. Additionally, because researchers in the 1960s and 1970s used methods that were deeply embedded in inferential statistics, their findings suggested that the effects of learning in one classroom would predictably affect students a similar way in all classrooms. By performing highly controlled experiments in school classrooms, students and their teachers became like so many rats in a maze, and educational researchers were watching isolated teacher and student behaviors like hawks from above and then analyzing these behaviors ad infinitum. Mostly lacking from these hawk-eye studies, however, were controls for cultural complexity, biases of the educators, prejudices of the learners, and other human qualities that are an integral part of the learning environment.

Much has changed during the past few decades. Now, there is inclusion, pluralistic teaching, transformative teaching, multiple perspectives, multicultural curricula, cognitive psychology, constructivist teaching strategies, cooperative team learning, urban schools, English as a Second Language, and so on. Whereas 20 years ago only a few first languages were spoken by students in school, there are now some schools in which more than 30 languages are represented. Clearly, the world has changed demographically and culturally, and it continues to do so at a staggering rate. Despite these radical changes, there remains a strong tendency for our schools to maintain traditional perspectives that have become comfortable, even if they are obsolete and irrelevant. Habit, tradition, and complacency are truly formidable barriers. Rituals, once in place, seem impervious to alterations. What people like about them, after all, is their sameness—their predictability.

In the face of demographic and corresponding cultural changes that are sweeping communities and their schools across the continent, plain common sense tells us that the old style of teaching, in which one size of instruction and one style of curriculum fits all students, just does not work anymore. Generalizable research theory in education, when combined with industrial ritualization of schools, is failing some groups of students. Year after year, blacks, Hispanics, Native Americans, and other minorities who do not adapt to the old-style uniformity of instruction and the industrialized educational ideologies come out on the short end of the mainstream educational measuring stick.

What does all this say about our educational system? It seems evident that some student groups are being kept perpetually on the lower rungs of the learning ladder; others, especially some groups of new immigrants, are adding rungs to the top of the ladder; and others, particularly members of white middle-class America, do not seem to care who is on the top or the bottom as long as it does not affect their standing.

If the general educational community is truly concerned about the social, academic, and financial future of our country, then it must be concerned about what is happening in our schools. We must raise eyebrows over young women, regardless of social class, ethnicity, or family background, being socialized out of science and mathematics in middle and high school; we must do more than give lip service to the marginalization of some student groups in our schools—namely, blacks, Hispanics, and Native Americans, among others; and we must learn lessons from many new immigrants who are moving educational standards, particularly in science and mathematics, to new heights.

Many of the old rituals, found in traditional school settings, do not work anymore. Why, then, are we so stubbornly and tenaciously holding onto them? One reason is that traditional schools are run like industrial factories in the cultural tradition of greater efficiency. This has taken priority over instructional effectiveness, much less the beauty and grace of our efforts.

Industrialization of School Rituals

Examine, for a moment, the origin of industrialized schooling, and examine the rituals that go with it, to see how our school system has become malfunctional and how it is underserving many of our students. The rituals in schools carry a certain power to communicate purposes and intentions that align with industrial-like values, including emotional, cultural, and social ideologies (Lesko, 1988).

What does all this mean for the school around the corner from your house? Also, what does this mean for the school you might be working in? Many educators today are working in turn-of-the-century institutions, and they carry with them a certain structure, a certain discourse, a certain kind of production level, and a certain way of interacting with others. This also means that if you now work in these environments, and if you attended these types of schools when you were growing up, then turn-of-the-century instructional habits, customs, and values are embedded deep within your perspectives of teaching and learning. Let's examine what this means for the kid next door who goes to the school just down the block and who is growing up in a fast-paced, pluralistic, technological society that has given rise to a global youth culture.

Schools are filled with ringing bells marking the beginning and ending of various events—the beginning of a class period, the tardy bell for beginning the school day, or the last bell of the day letting everyone go home for the evening. Bells represent fire alarms and tornado alerts as well. Maybe you know from firsthand experience what happens when you are in the wrong place when a school bell goes off. When this happened to you, did you get punished? Did you get demerits? Were you sent to a special time-out place in the school? Just where does all this tradition (punishment, demerits, and tardy bells) come from? How does it all fit into the idea of ritualization of schools?

For a more realistic picture of industrialized rituals of schools, consider the play *Cheaper by the Dozen,* which was made into a movie of the same name. This is a story about a family of 12 children that was "managed" efficiently and economically by a father who ran his home like a factory—everything by the clock. All family events began and ended on time. Each morning, precisely 20 minutes after the wake-up alarm had sounded, the father would stand at the foot of the stairway with a stopwatch and blow a loud whistle. All 12 children would immediately begin running downstairs and line up from the oldest to the youngest. As soon as the children lined up and stood at attention, the father would stop the watch and give them an efficiency rating. This was how the father, who was an efficiency expert employed by a factory, managed his family.

This story takes a satirical and humorous look at how industrial life, and scientific management of factories, overtook so many aspects of our lives. Although we might laugh out loud and shake our heads at the absurdity of managing a family by the clock, this is exactly what has happened in many of our schools. Clocks, bells, and efficient flow of students from one part of the school building to another all have become mainstays in our schools. So have many other aspects of industrial life, including obedience to culture, subservience to authority, and strict compliance to rules and regulations.

There is something else about the industrialized nature of schools, however, that is now calling their rituals into question. Industrial organizations were (and remain) organized around capitalist ideologies. The people who had the most money—for example, the owners of the factory—were those who had the greatest power and, consequently, the final word on matters. Their wishes, their ideologies, and their visions were the ones that became the factory culture. The middle managers were the ones who were expected to safeguard the culture by managing and controlling the actions, thoughts, and productivity of the workers.

Moreover, factories, especially those at the turn of the century, were overshadowed by white middle-class values and had very specific gender role expectations: Men did heavy work and women did secretarial chores. The message that came out of these early factories was that "real" work, that which has the most meaning and the most value, is done by men, is managed by men, and is owned by men. Not just any men, but white middle-class managers and white upper-class owners.

When we look at schools this way, we can see a certain historical structure, power hierarchy, discourse, way of thinking, and expected level of productivity: All these things are overshadowed by the idea of careful, efficient management to ensure the "largest dividend upon the material investment of time, energy, and money" (Bagley, 1907). Schools have been quick to adopt strategies such as management by objectives, total quality management, and so on. All this corporate envy that schools cling to seems harmless, and perhaps some of it is even beneficial. This might have been true for the early 1900s, especially if your background, your lifestyle, and your values all aligned with factory ways of thinking—in the case of North American factories, this was mostly Eurocentric middle-class ways of thinking (Fine, 1991).

In a critical look at this industrial model of schooling, Bullough (1994) describes principals as managers who are in charge of making the system run without a hitch. Teachers are factory workers on the assembly line, perhaps semiskilled at best, who are responsible for meeting production goals such as stanine scores, body counts, and percentage of graduates. Students are simply products that are shaped, molded, and, in some cases, stapled and mutilated to get them in and out quietly and efficiently. Any defective material is simply shipped off somewhere else.

This analogy is highly appropriate for many of today's schools. What if your social class, your cultural heritage, your values for learning, your beliefs about power and authority, your family background and culture, and your interactions with peers—all of which translate into value-laden rituals—do not necessarily align with the kind of industrialized factory-like thinking described previously? What if your social philosophy and your social perspective misalign with a factory view of schooling? What if, as a student or a parent, your ritualized ways of knowing are mismatched with the ritualized ways of middle-class factory life, with its emphasis on obedience to mainstream cultural values, on hard predictable work, on valuing efficiency, on competition, on winning and losing, and on compliant and somewhat passive team work? Then what? Too bad for you.

On a pragmatic level, we might wonder what is so wrong with the factory metaphor. It is efficient. It is cost-effective. It keeps things running smoothly. It gives us informed, educated persons for maintaining and upholding our society. This model, however, does not provide for those who do not necessarily fit the assembly line mold. The ritual of academic tracking, with its emphasis on graded learning and efficient transmission of content, does not necessarily facilitate equity and excellence (Gay, 1988).

Becoming Ritualized

Have you ever visited another country, or region of this country, where the customs, language, values, and religion were completely new to you? How did you feel when you first arrived there? If you were a tourist in this other country, did you happen to get lost as you walked around a town or city or when you drove through the countryside? Did you panic when you were lost, thinking you might not find your way back from where you started? Did you think that someone might take advantage of you and try to give you directions that would take you to yet another lost destination? If you went to another country to live rather than being a tourist, how many months passed before you became comfortable with the surroundings? Did you learn just enough of the local language to get by in the marketplace or did you really try to become a proficient speaker of the local language? Finally, when you returned home from visiting another country, how did you feel when you were once again on familiar ground?

Imagine what it must feel like for your students when they move to a new school in which the language, customs, values, and peers are all different from anything they have ever experienced. All this newness would likely give them an overwhelming feeling of being alone and at the same time make them feel like they are really standing out in the crowd. These feelings are, of course, quite natural; they are a very real part of becoming familiar with new cultural terrain.

After you have been to a new place for a while, you begin to become familiar with local customs, and part of your life begins to be shaped by the ritualized lives of others you are around; the feelings of extreme loneliness and cultural awkwardness slowly begin to go away. This process, however, can involve much struggle and pain. In school settings and communities in which kids and their parents can be so resistant to new cultural rituals, a "new kid on the block," especially one from another country, can be pushed to the edge of school life very quickly.

This process of being pushed to the most dilapidated part of the assembly line occurs through being separated from others at first. Next comes a second phase of being ritualized, called *liminality*, in which confusion dominates as the person tries to reconcile previous customs with new ones. Turner (1966, 1992) likens this to a death-like state in which the person is stripped of personal attributes to make room for new ones. Naturally, this would produce a degree of humiliation, destruction, and degradation in a person. Finally, in the third phase, *aggregation*, a person has adopted a new way of life, utterly transformed into an alien being his or her family would hardly recognize.

These three aspects of ritualization can be applied easily to the ethnographic work of Wilson (1991) with Sioux Indian high school students. Indian students, who are used to attending elementary schools that have integrated familiar cultural rituals into daily activities, are suddenly placed in a mainstream high school in which the patterns are quite different. The approach to learning at the mainstream high school, the interactions with peers and teachers, and the social expectations in classroom dialogue involve new dynamics for learning.

At first glance, you might imagine the Sioux students should become acclimated to their new learning environment after a few weeks. Surely they are young enough to adapt to the assembly line just like everyone else. For some reason, however, 8 of 10 elected not to become part of this system; they dropped out of school prior to graduation.

Teachers viewed the Sioux students as neophytes in school— as mostly empty slates needing to be filled with the "correct" habits of thinking, ways of speaking, and ways of interacting with others in and out of the classroom. These rituals, however, may be correct for mainstream school life but may not be suitable for others outside the mainstream. This clearly happened with the Sioux 10th-grade students.

The high school teachers who taught the Sioux students report-edly discounted the reservation schools and misjudged the quality of their education rather than contextualizing the education within a ritualized school context of Native American culture. Conse-quently, the teachers held firmly to their own ritualized school lives, expecting the Native American students to strip away their cultural ways of knowing and learning that they acquired over many years in reservation schools. Then, the teachers expected the Sioux students to immediately apply new ways of learning and adopt new class-room rituals. To do this, the Native American students had to dis-mantle their previous status as viable learners in reservation schools and temper their personal essence as Sioux Indians so that they would presumably be better prepared, according to mainstream teachers, to cope with their high school responsibilities.

Using Turner's (1966) description of liminality, which is the period of time when persons new to a culture are viewed as being "in the womb," teachers likely viewed them as a form of "clay" so that they could be more easily molded and shaped by the rituals of mainstream schooling. The students, however, did not want to be, nor need to be, reshaped by mainstream rituals of schooling. Also, they assuredly did not want to be viewed as death-like creatures who, if given the nutrients of mainstream education, would then grow into the right kind of educated person. The high school teachers, however, with their lack of understanding of ritualized life at Native American schools and with their lack of empathy for what the Sioux students were experiencing as they were involuntarily separated from their familiar school rituals and then plopped into mainstream school life, contributed to this. Perhaps the Sioux Indian students, at least the 80% who dropped out during their first year of mainstream school-ing, elected to retain their Native American ways of understanding the world around them. By being pushed to the margins of school life early in their mainstream school experience, these Sioux students never even arrived at Turner's aggregation stage of ritualization—a phase in which the students would have adopted, internalized, and begun to demonstrate mainstream school rituals.

Although we are reframing, perhaps even romanticizing, the Indian students' pride, the reality for most of them will be that without completing their education, they will be relegated to the bottom of the economic ladder throughout their lifetimes. They may hold on to their cultural rituals but will do so at a very dear price.

Toward a New Social Imagination
for Schooling

It is very easy to sit back, analyze the actions of teachers in one school context, and then pass judgment as to what is right and what is wrong, all in the name of equity and justice. Surely anyone who reads about educational injustices like these, however unintentional, comes away feeling angry, incensed, and annoyed. It is equally easy, however, to become defensive if you are one of the teachers being criticized for being insensitive and unresponsive to some students. You say, "What's wrong with the way I teach? I have all these kids. I can't be expected to teach each one a different way. There would be chaos."

What we have argued in this chapter is that one reason why students such as the Sioux Indians leave school is because the ritualized ways of knowing in many schools reflect mainstream values, behaviors, and expectations. These ways of knowing, however, are not all bad. In fact, these rituals are very important in bringing people together for common causes, for universal purposes, and for shared identities. When rituals are so firmly entrenched and inflexible, however, then there is little room for others with alternative ways of knowing, with other subjectivities, to move around comfortably. The discomfort becomes too great, so they leave—either physically or emotionally and spiritually—as empty, listless minds.

The main question that surfaces from this discussion is how can we open our schools, with their industrialized rituals, to alternative ways of knowing so that students do not leave, so that they feel like they are part of the system, and so that they are not pushed to the margins? How can we, as an educational community, see *who* students are and not *what* they are?

The problem for teachers then becomes one of moving beyond their own ritualized perspectives of factory-like schooling, and the teaching habits that come with these perspectives, to accommodate other perspectives. The following are a couple of ways to do this, and each method requires proactive and reflective thinking about teaching: (a) expanding social imagination and (b) taking purposeful social action in the classroom.

Expanding your social imagination means opening your heart and mind to new ways of interacting with others, not only as a mechanical exercise but also as a way of seeing the world around you.

By doing this, you enter into dialogue with others, sharing your perspective with them, and, it is hoped, building an understanding of their perspective. This gives you alternative ways of being with your students and enriches social relationships in your classroom. Expanding your social imagination also relates to possibilities, specifically, those of reaching beyond where you are with respect to those around you (Greene, 1994). This means that you have to know where you are and who you are; then you have to know those around you, and you must know who they are and not only what they are. Then you can come to know how to reach beyond your own ritualized ways of knowing. This is one way to avoid stripping away the subjectivities of others and, at the same time, build solidarity among your students.

Preliminal and postliminal attributes of your students can then add beauty and cultural richness to your learning environment. The culture within all students is affirmed, engaged, shared, and broadened as you bring their ritualized ways of knowing collectively to the learning moment.

For example, a group of Hispanic parents approached a teacher complaining that she celebrated Columbus Day and Presidents' Day in her classes but not Cinco de Mayo. Defensive at first, she reminded them of school policy that stated that they simply could not celebrate every ethnic holiday; there would not be enough days in the year. Then she began thinking about the beauty and grace of these rituals and how they could easily be adapted to whatever lessons she was teaching. During one math lesson, she introduced a whole discussion of cultural systems of numbering from Roman and Arabic systems to other less-known models.

The second way to move beyond factory-like rituals is to demonstrate purposeful social action in the classroom. These changes must happen by design—by purposeful action (see Apple & Beane, 1995). For example, Davidson (1994) describes the kind of dialogue that can emerge from penetrating explorations in which young people examine the sociocultural messages they receive from their families, peer groups, and schools. Ideally, they would critically review those values, interactive patterns, rules, and expectations that are most meaningful and useful as well as those that are most limiting.

For example, during one conversation with Carla, a Latina student, Davidson (1994, p. 158) attempted to help her define some of the parameters of her school culture and rituals: "In terms of people here at school, what kinds of expectations do teachers and administrators have of people of your background?"

Carla responded very quickly that they do not expect Latinos to do as well academically. "They probably expect a lot of us to drop out, not to graduate. I think they expect most of us to have babies" (p. 158).

Carla is pressed further to translate vague feelings into a more detailed analysis of what various people in her life expect of her. She is helped to reflect on the origins of her beliefs and, more important, what she can do to alter these narratives. In this form of cultural therapy, devised by Spindler and Spindler (1990, 1994), Carla is encouraged to make explicit the hidden agendas and forces, as well as explicit school rituals, that make her job of learning quite challenging. It was hoped that she would be helped to resolve the inevitable cultural conflicts that coexist within every student. Unfortunately, this is a process that takes time.

Accommodating Student Rituals

When you stop to think about rituals as we have done in this chapter, then you begin to see why purposeful action is needed before real change can happen. Every one of your actions at school can be placed in a ritualized framework, and the framework has form, structure, boundaries, values, ideals, expectations, and rules. The more you work within this framework, the more you become habituated to it. This habituation, in turn, limits your perspective, holds your social imagination in check, and causes you to co-opt others into your framework. In fact, we tend to feel mighty annoyed when students challenge our system and demonstrate forcefully that they do not wish to be part of our assembly line.

What you, as a professional educator, have truly learned about your students will be apparent in the daily decisions you make about engaging every one of them, as individual human beings and not as stereotypical members of groups and categories, in the learning process. A key feature to making these decisions is discernment—knowing what to do and say at the right classroom moment and knowing what not to do (Powell, Zehm, & Garcia, 1996).

That our society has become increasingly diverse in so many ways is a reality that we all must deal with. Schools, too, must cope with this challenge, but they remain entrenched in a factory-like whirr of efficiency. Unless schools begin adjusting to the emergence of a global community, and unless educators expand their social imagination and agree to enrich the web of relationships, schools will remain places of learning for only an increasingly smaller percentage of the population. This is already happening: The school drop-out rate, according to national statistics, has never been higher in the history of our country.

Making students' cultural rituals an integral part of your classroom teaching may not be the only solution to the disconnections that many students are now feeling toward school, but it is one way to think about correcting the misalignment between students and traditional school settings. This requires constant vigilance—an ongoing discernment that alerts you when traditional rituals are constraining and when they are fostering students' engagement with you, with other students, and with content you expect them to learn. Factory-like schooling, with its deeply entrenched rituals associated with learning and behaving, its narrow definitions of student success and achievement, and its myriad of student labels, dichotomies, and categories obscures the diversities, subjectivities, and, consequently, the beauty and grace of students' ritualized lives outside of school.

Bridge

Teaching as if You Were
an Anthropologist

This chapter represents a bridge between the provocative ideas presented in Part I of the book and some constructive applications of these concepts to the realities of teaching practice presented in Part II. Before examining how we might do things differently in our classrooms, we will first examine an alternative way of thinking about our work. This conceptual shift may very well alter how we think about our jobs as well as change both the tone and the content of our dialogues with colleagues in the teachers' lounge.

The Culture of an Anthropologist

A real anthropologist's life probably is not nearly as exciting as you might imagine.

There she is, sitting around a campfire, wearing a tribal outfit, acting like she is one of the gang. You can tell she is accepted among them because they occasionally pat her on the back and she knows their secret handshake. She chatters away in the native language as if it is her own.

Her eyes are bright, as if she is seeing something that few of her kind have ever seen before, some mystical rite that explains the origins of the universe or certainly the history of this particular people. You can see that she is trying hard to memorize every detail of the scene, privileged as she is to be a participant in this rare experience. She seems so alive, transcended, transported from her own world to this other one that is so different. Even more impressive is that she seems so at ease. She has somehow adapted to this strange place and people, become totally open to their experience in such a way that she can function as a participant and observer without judging them, without making comparisons to what she is used to, and without feeling threatened, annoyed, or unduly disturbed by cultural practices that are so alien to her senses.

Later, when she does reflect on her experiences immersed in another culture, she is amused by the seemingly infinite number of ways that human beings have developed to conduct the daily affairs of their existence. Eating is only one example that comes to mind. There are not only at least a dozen different cultural practices related to how one eats—for example, with fingers, fork, chopsticks, or banana leaves—but also many different products that various peoples will eat, or not eat, as the case may be. Some cultural practices prohibit eating cows (India), pigs (Middle East), or domesticated dogs and cats (North America). Others regard foods that one might consider abhorrent to be the ultimate delicacy—for example, spiders, rats, monkeys, or eagles. How interesting, the anthropologist muses, that humans are so amazingly adaptable and inventive in how they organize their lives.

I skip the part of the anthropologist's life that is usually left out during fictionalized or documentary accounts of some famous field scientist who has made a breakthrough discovery in the wilds. This is the part in which during most of her travels she struggled with dysentery, open sores, and a persistent parasite that has yet to be identified; the part in which she felt lonely, uncomfortable, and afraid some of the time; the part in which she went to sleep with a headache on the hard ground on most nights, trying to decipher much of what was witnessed; the part in which she plotted and planned how she would get herself out of debt after this adventure; and the part in which she worried incessantly about the relationships she had left behind.

I also leave out the part of the anthropologist's job that is hardly glamorous. This includes the hundreds of hours she will spend writing her field notes and coding her "data"; the ridicule she will suffer by colleagues who are jealous of what she is trying to accomplish; the political struggles she will face getting her work published; and the 60-hour weeks she will spend taking care of her other responsibilities—serving on university committees, advising students, preparing her classes, delivering lectures, reading papers, and grading exams. All the while, she tries to scrape together funding sources for her next expedition into the unknown.

So why, you might ask, would I ever suggest that a teacher, or anyone else for that matter, adopt the role of a anthropologist?

Alternative Teacher Roles

Many teachers are prepared to function as junior psychologists. We learned the stages of evolution that people go through on their path toward maturity in our earliest courses about child development. We were indoctrinated into psychological theories of cognitive development, moral development, physical development, emotional development, and gender identity. We were schooled in the mechanisms by which human beings learn things, how memory works, and how best to get inside children's minds and hearts so that we can teach them things we think they should know.

We are comfortable in our role as psychologists. If we are not proficient in the skills, we are at least familiar with their intent—to diagnose problems, assess individual strengths and weaknesses, devise interventions, and measure changes in performance. Teacher-as-psychologist is a role that encourages us to use our helping skills to understand children's experience, to relate to them as individuals, and to influence them through strategies of behavior management.

Brandon has a reputation in his school for having the most obedient students and the most orderly classroom. Children know just what is expected. If they step out of line, they know exactly what will follow. Every behavior, whether constructive or distracting, has a specific consequence. Things proceed in an orderly way. If someone should deviate from expected norms, Brandon is highly skilled at figuring out the motive behind the behavior, what the child is really wanting, and how to get him or her back on track.

Do not get me wrong: I think this is quite a legitimate and effective professional identity for teachers to adopt. Such a role encourages us to look at the underlying meaning of a child's behavior, to discover how it is being reinforced by others, and to devise ways to change behavioral patterns to fit more appropriate classroom demeanor.

Likewise, the role of teacher as instructional designer is one that is both common and useful. This is when we see ourselves as responsible for identifying content to be mastered, curricula to be devised, and instructional plans to be implemented. In other words, we see the child as being essentially empty, an entity just waiting to be filled up with all the good stuff we have to offer.

Like Brandon, Louise is also highly organized. Whereas he is concerned with the psychological ramifications of behavior—his own as well as that of his students—Louise is more concerned with developing a content-rich curricula. She invests most of her energy into designing varied lesson plans, incorporating learning strategies that maximize student involvement on multiple levels, and constructing reliable and valid tests to measure progress. Also like Brandon, Louise is damn good at what she does.

If these two types of professional orientations for a teacher are both effective, why develop a third one, especially one that involves adopting the perspective of a field scientist?

What It Means to
Be an Anthropologist

Margaret Mead (1927) advocated as early as the 1920s that training in anthropology should be required for teachers to help them become more flexible and to step outside themselves in an effort to appreciate the unique experiences of others. She also believed that one of a teacher's primary jobs is to help children make constructive use of their cultural inheritance (Monroe, 1992).

Anthropologists offer a balance in their perspective that is often missing through the lenses of psychologists or instructional designers. Rather than focusing on individual motivation and behavior, or on the content of teaching, an anthropological approach to schooling would be most concerned with the cultural practices of people. Anthropologists are interested not only in children's behavior in school but also in the knowledge base they share with others of their social group that leads them to think, feel, and act as they do (Grant & Sleeter, 1986). Of course, this particular perspective is just as limited as any other I might mention—a teacher who is concerned exclusively with discipline and control of student behavior, a teacher who addresses only children's emotional needs while neglecting their academic achievement, or a teacher who adopts any particular discipline or theoretical orientation to the exclusion of others.

Margaret Mead (1927) championed anthropological principles in schools by advocating the relativity of all cultures and the basic equality of all people (Perlmutter, 1992). Subsequently, her remarks have been misinterpreted by some to mean that she was advocating that all cultures should be treated equally rather than equally treated with respect and legitimate solutions to life's problems (G. Spindler, personal communication, 1996).

Sowell (1994) is aghast at what he claims is the dishonest, inaccurate, and neglectful way that academics, journalists, and others have taken the anthropological notion of cultural relativity to an extreme. Part of the politically correct landscape is that we are not allowed to speak about the superiority of some cultures over others in specific areas. It is obvious, however, that the Arabic numerical system is far better than the one invented by Romans, or that guns have proven to be far more effective as instruments of hunting and war than bows and arrows.

Despite some disadvantages of anthropology as a guiding field for the teacher—notably, its emphasis on group behavior and cultural practices while downplaying individual behavior and biological forces—it has much to offer as another means by which to make sense of what is happening in our classrooms. Most of all, anthropologists honor those parts of the larger community, both past and present, that influence a person's behavior.

There are several implications for a teacher who decides to function as an anthropologist in addition to functioning in other roles that are routinely adopted. Above all else, such a teacher would be a student of culture—that is, impassioned and curious about the origins of social behavior. The following questions might repeatedly come to mind:

- What is it about where this student comes from that leads him or her to respond to others the way he or she does?
- What is it that I do not know or understand about this child's background that might help me make sense of what is happening?
- How might I investigate further the customs of this child's family?
- What are the interactive effects of having so many cultures represented in this classroom?
- How are my cultural values and biases getting in the way of honoring those among my students that are different from what I am used to?

Questions such as these arise from certain assumptions that are part of the anthropologist's style of thinking. Jacob (1995) advocates an anthropological perspective for the teacher that encourages more careful examination of the cultural context of all behavior. Jacob describes a number of breakthroughs that occurred as a direct result of this approach. Jacob contends that merely learning about cultures is hardly enough because general information may hardly be relevant to particular community microcultures. By combining the work of Schon (1983, 1987) on reflective practice with a solid anthropological foundation, Jacob suggests following several steps when confronted with a puzzling situation in the classroom.

Define the Puzzlement

Construct a personal definition of the problem based on personal observations and experience. Of course, if the particular "framing" of the problem gets in the way, you can use a device borrowed from the therapy profession known as "reframing," in which the problem is redefined in a more constructive way. For example, if labeling a child's behavior as "obstructive" leads you to feel angry, frustrated, and challenged, then reframing that same behavior as "asking for attention" helps you to feel more neutral. It is far easier to respond to someone who is asking for attention than it is to someone you believe is trying to hurt you in some way.

Reflect Deeply on the Situation

If you reframe surprises in your classroom as opportunities for you to learn and grow, then such predicaments become less noxious and even potentially welcome. By functioning as an anthropologist rather than as a psychologist or instructional designer, you are not so much trying to make sense of the child's inner motivation, or what went wrong with your teaching strategy, as you are trying to understand the cultural contexts for what took place within the child, within the other students, and within the culture in you.

If, for example, you examine the impact of the competitive culture you have created in your class through your grading system, you can begin to figure out what meaning that has for each child, given his or her own cultural contexts. For example, to Kim, one of the Hong Kong students in your class, the competition you have set up is both familiar and comfortable to her. She likes knowing where she stands in relation to all others. Without such external pressure, which has been a part of her life since birth, she would struggle terribly. Likewise, for Salustio, who attended private schools in Mexico City while in his early years and is part of a highly successful family of real estate brokers, competitive cultures are not only fine with him but also necessary for him to function effectively. Kyle, however, comes from ethnic origins that are part Native American, a religious upbringing that has emphasized cooperation over competition, and a family culture that stresses not doing anything that would belittle anyone else. Although extremely bright and capable, she refuses to participate in a system she finds not only foreign to her experience but also absolutely the antithesis of all she has learned.

Because the behavior you find puzzling is why Kyle will not turn in her assignments, you are now able to understand that she is not challenging your authority nor is she lazy and stupid; rather, she is struggling with her own culture, which is at odds with the culture that you have constructed in your classroom.

It is during this reflective process that you assess each student's level and style of cultural adaption. On the basis of their study of Menominee Indians located in Wisconsin, Spindler and Spindler

(1984) developed a typology to account for differences in how Native American children adapt to mainstream culture that they later evolved into a type of "cultural therapy" (Spindler & Spindler, 1994). This involves the process by which people come to understand their own culture in relation to the traditions and values of others.

Thinking like an anthropologist, Trueba (1993) developed this model to further explain why some minority children in our schools function much more comfortably than others and why some become behavior problems, whereas others become model citizens.

Given that anthropologists are students of the bigger picture, the goal is to explain various responses to cultural conflict that are inevitable when people must adapt to worlds that are foreign to their upbringing and experience. There are basically four kinds of responses possible for minority students who are trying to deal with mainstream culture that is dominant in school.

Nativistic reactions are represented by the extreme position that one's own culture, language, and customs must be preserved at all costs, even if it means outright rejection of everything associated with the dominant culture. Children following this position would be perceived as isolated and hostile to any attempt to help them become involved in school activities. They are doing everything within their power to maintain their own cultural heritage in its purest form. They are not so much trying to disrupt your class or get underneath your skin as they are trying to protect themselves from perceived threats: They feel you are trying to strip them of their culture (and they are right).

Transitional responses are a more neutral cultural strategy. The student adopts a wait-and-see attitude: "Let's see how this all unfolds—I will watch and see what the consequences are for others who take one position or another, then I will commit myself to my own course of action." Although such students may appear to teachers as passive or disengaged, their cognitive processes may be quite active as they form their own judgments. Like the nativistic position, and the assimilationist position that follows, the student does not feel secure enough in his or her own cultural heritage to make the kinds of compromises that are necessary for true personal integration.

Assimilationist responses can be just as self-destructive as the nativistic position, although a student using this response will hardly give you trouble. Rather than rejecting the mainstream culture outright, the student distances himself or herself from his or her own culture. The student refuses to acknowledge his or her cultural roots and instead jumps into the dominant culture as if it was always his or her own. The student will be accepted most easily by teachers and majority students, but he or she may pay a dear price in disowning his or her background.

Multicultural strategies are considered to be the ideal position in that the student is able to reconcile the conflicting pushes and pulls of the home culture versus the school culture. Such a student is very motivated to learn as much as he or she can about mainstream customs and language but also retains pride in his or her own culture.

Obviously, it is this fourth type of cultural adaption that is usually considered optimal because the student learns to integrate mainstream cultural practices into native customs. Depending on your assessment of where a student is regarding the previously described responses, your job would be to help facilitate a strategy in which students can integrate their past with the present and their home culture with the school culture.

Develop and Implement an Intervention

It is not as if you can simply say to yourself about Kyle: "Okay, competition doesn't fit with her experience so I'll just make allowances for her that I would not for the others that quite like my system." Even if such a strategy were possible, you would hardly be doing Kyle a service. Throughout her life, she is going to have to learn how to reconcile her culture with the realities of the world, a larger culture in which functioning under competitive pressure is not only desirable but also crucial for even reasonable success in life.

From the reflection you have undertaken, you also consider the implications of your classroom culture for Kim, Salustio, and the rest of your students. Are you really doing them a service by reinforcing so strongly the values of competition? Many of your students do not feel the slightest intrinsic desire to learn; everything they do is for some reward, whether it be your approval or the satisfaction of scoring higher than others. Now you wonder if Kyle is not the one with her head most clear. Maybe there are some changes you can make in how you structure your class so that Kyle can learn the valuable lessons that Kim and Salustio have mastered and that Kim and Salustio can learn the importance of Kyle's culture, which stresses doing things for fun rather than for external rewards. Maybe it is about time they learned about the negative side effects of an achievement orientation.

Anthropological interventions can take place on many levels. For example, changes can be made in the instructional context in which Hispanic students who previously functioned quite low in their English reading skills can be allowed to read in Spanish to demonstrate their abilities (Moll & Diaz, 1993). Another option involves altering the social and power structure of the classroom by inviting minority parents to have more input and involvement in what goes on at school. In one such experiment, the parents of Mexican American children were invited to form their own committee charged with educating the school about their cultural needs and helping other Mexican families learn about the school culture (Delgado-Gaitan, 1990). In other programs described by Ladson-Billings (1994) in her work with African American children, attempts are made to include real-life experiences as legitimate components of the official curriculum.

Throughout each of these three steps in the process, the teacher is encouraged to focus not on the problems that result from cultural encounters but on the advantages of such variability. After all, during our tenure on this planet, it has been through the interactions between cultures, whether through trade, intermarriage, exchanges, or even conquest, that human culture has evolved. Those cultures that have remained most isolated, whether in Lapland, New Guinea, Afghanistan, or Central Africa, have suffered the most in terms of advancement and adaptability.

Isolation of a culture eventually leads to death, or at least terminal stagnation. It is by interacting with members of different cultures that we are able to learn alternative ways of viewing the world and of applying what we already know in more innovative ways. Therefore, it is one of the central roles of the teacher as anthropologist to facilitate the exchange of cultural ideas.

Studying culture means reading about worlds that are different from what we are used to. With every novel we read and every film we see, there is a window into the world of people who live differently than we do. Vicariously, we are experiencing other cultures without actually getting carsick. As safe and sanitized as such mind travels might be, they help us to open our eyes and hearts to human practices that initially appear quite strange.

Anthropologists try hard not to judge the behavior of the people they are studying. Although it is extremely difficult not to form opinions about the relative merits of waging war, enforcing laws, preparing foods, or throwing a party in particular ways, such a neutral posture helps to approach all cultural practices as "interesting" rather than "disgusting," "weird," or "stupid."

It is because I have studied the cultural practices of some Native American tribes that I was able to recognize that what might have been happening with one of my students was not what it appeared to be.

Sylvia had been an excellent student. Quiet and reserved, as is often typical for others of her tribe, she was dedicated to her studies and highly motivated to do well. Because her attendance had previously been excellent, I was surprised that one day she simply disappeared. No phone call. No explanation. Not wanting to intrude, I waited to see if she would return.

My first reaction was one of anger: What an irresponsible action on her part!—and from a student I had mistakenly thought really cared about her studies. I thought to myself, "I don't care if she is Indian or not, there is no excuse for simply leaving class without the courtesy of an explanation."

Then I realized that I was probably missing something. Just because I would handle things in a particular way, given my cultural background, does not mean that others are used to the same rules. I now felt quite curious about what had happened. Certainly, I was concerned about Sylvia, but I was also intrigued by what phenomenon was transpiring.

I began a series of investigations of a general nature about what might cause a student to "disappear" from class. I did some reading on the subject, spoke with several other teachers, and confided my concerns to a few other students with whom I enjoyed a trusting relationship. They were also puzzled about what happened to Sylvia but felt it was none of their business.

Finally, I took the most obvious action of all—the one I should have thought of first: I asked another Indian student if he knew what happened to Sylvia. He smiled shyly and nodded his head. I waited for him to tell me more but he just stood there with his eyes flitting toward my feet. "Well?" I demanded a little too stridently, my impatience and frustration slipping through. Very casually, he then proceeded to explain that among his people, when there is a death in the extended family, it is expected that close relatives will spend a year in mourning. This often involves dropping out of their usual activities so that they can devote their time and efforts full time to honoring the person's departed spirit.

I thought this was weird—not at all like an anthropologist would think. I immediately considered all the aspects of this ritual that seemed so impractical and unreasonable. If something tragic happened in my family, how the hell could I ever quit my job and . . . wait a minute! There was something I was missing: Why didn't she tell me what had happened or why she was leaving? I could almost understand her need to handle things according to the ways of her people, but a little courtesy would have been appreciated—certainly notification that she would not be returning.

The young man smiled shyly and stated, "It is not up to her to tell you about her loss; it is up to you to ask."

Wow! That was absolutely mind-blowing.

Thinking like an anthropologist now, I considered an alternative reality, one in which the rules that I am most familiar with do not apply. This student was not being irresponsible at all; she was simply doing what was expected of her by the members of her family and tribe. Even more intriguing, part of the cultural rules is that she is not allowed to tell others about her grief; others are supposed to care enough to find out.

Time and time again, the study of cultures through books, movies, and conversations serves us well in being able to recognize differences in people and the infinite number of ways they have learned to respond to various circumstances in life. Vicarious experiences such as these are wonderfully educational in expanding our horizons and challenging our most cherished assumptions about the world, but they are no substitute for actual experience immersed in foreign cultures.

Traveling Like an Anthropologist

I have long been fascinated by how, through structured immersion experiences, dramatic transformations are promoted in how people think, feel, and behave. As a therapist and counselor educator, I have been frustrated by how long my profession takes to make a difference in people's lives; psychotherapy and counseling are often extremely time-consuming.

What if someone was in a hurry and wanted to change his or her outlook on life rather quickly? What if a person wished to dramatically alter his or her perceptions of himself or herself and the world? What if a teacher wanted to change how he or she thinks about his or her work in such a way that he or she would be far more sensitive and responsive to cultural diversity? Would I recommend therapy, even the kind of cultural therapy developed by George and Louise Spindler that helps people to look at issues of dominance, oppression, and power?

The answer is most probably no. The truth is that nothing changes a person's outlook on life more dramatically and quickly than an experience that places him or her in a different culture in which he or she can no longer rely on usual modes of functioning. In work in this area (Kottler, 1997b), I described a number of individuals who changed their lives as a result of a particular kind of travel in which they faced a number of challenges that forced them to create new ways to think about what it means to be a teacher and a human being.

If you really were interested in becoming far more flexible and creative in your life and work, how might you structure a travel experience to promote significant growth?

Much of travel is a staged phenomenon—a contrived series of events that are made to look authentic but, on closer examination, are really part of a show. We willingly suspend disbelief so that we may enjoy the world as one big Disneyland—nature harnessed for our entertainment and culture manipulated for maximum effect.

I once traveled deep into the Amazon jungle to catch a glimpse of local culture in its natural, primitive state. After flying to a town in Northern Peru, we boarded a small boat for the trip down the Amazon and then along a tributary to a remote lodge. The next morning, we took an even smaller boat farther down the increasingly smaller stream until we could go no farther. We hiked for a few hours to a village where the locals, dressed in their grass skirts and head-hunter outfits, agreed to put on a demonstration of their blowgun shooting skills in exchange for a few cigarettes (we were told they had no concept of money). They showed us their primitive huts in which they lived and allowed us to watch them at work in their daily chores making reed flutes and bone fishhooks.

I wandered away from the village just to have a look around. I noticed sounds coming from a clearing and followed them until I came upon quite another scene: the real village where people actually lived when they were not performing for tourists. People were living in well-constructed, wood lodges and wearing cutoff jeans and T-shirts with Notre Dame and Nike logos.

The demonstration that we had witnessed was just like Disneyland—a well-orchestrated performance by professionals. Of course, if you do not look behind the scenes, or in this case behind the jungle, you would never know that your "adventure" is really just a tourist show.

It is the deceptive and manipulative aspect of this staged show for tourists that riles our cynicism. In other circumstances, however, we are more than grateful for efforts that have been made on our behalf. In national parks, for example, trails are clearly marked and rangers are on patrol to provide a reasonable degree of safety that might otherwise preclude expeditions to remote areas.

To a given individual, depending on expectations and previous experience, a contrived tourist event works just as well as one that is authentic—in some cases, even more so. The object, after all, is to get your heart beating quickly, to heighten your awareness and perception, and to influence you profoundly. For some people, a ride through a simulated Nile in the Luxor Hotel may indeed be something that is as educational and influential as the real thing.

Traveling like an anthropologist, however, means "going native"—getting away from sanitized experiences as much as you can so that you can feel what it is like to be part of another culture, with all its joys and contradictions. In one of the few systematic investigations of travel as a transformative experience, Leed (1991) concludes that it works because of its paradoxes—departures and arrivals, detachments and connection, and freedom and structure. It is a study of conflicts and needs in opposition to one another.

Consistently throughout the travel literature he reviewed, Leed (1991) found that journeys place the traveler in a zone of ambiguity and uncertainty, stripped away from the usual self to a transitional identity that is both freed and constrained. This paradox makes travel changes very difficult to understand and to plan for. Most stories in which people were changed significantly by a trip involve situations in which things went wrong—when they missed a flight, got lost, encountered a frightening situation, or overcame some significant challenge.

It is only after the adventure is over, when wounds are healed and memories become selective, that we romanticize and glorify what occurred. We portray ourselves as courageous, intrepid explorers, forging ahead in a spirit of good cheer. We forget the parts when we whined and complained, when we thought of turning back, and when we desperately wanted to be in the familiar comforts of our bed or bathtub instead of wandering lost in the bush or back alleys of some godforsaken place.

In *Tales of a Traveler*, Washington Irving commented that any change, even from bad to worse, brings about a certain relief. After being jostled around inside a stagecoach for hours on end, he observed that "it is often a comfort to shift one's position and be bruised in a new place."

"Nothing left to lose" is a refrain uttered by anyone who changes positions, literally or metaphorically, because even new bruises would be better than old ones that never heal. There is novelty, if not amusement, in discovering new ways you can hurt.

For example, at age 14, my son spent 3 months living with friends and going to school in New Zealand. It was the worst time of his life and also the very best. He was constantly homesick and lonely. Because he was often teased at school for being different, he also felt alienated. He lived in a home in which there was much conflict because his surrogate parents had decided to divorce. He felt deprived of the things he valued the most: his parents, his friends, baseball, and favorite foods. There were many nights he cried himself to sleep, counting the days, even the hours, until he could return home.

With all these hardships, however, there has never been a time in which he felt more stimulated: "I learned more in 3 months than I ever could back home, and not from school either." He learned to be more responsible and to deal with different situations he had never faced before. He began to appreciate that changes are fun—that playing rugby and cricket is a pleasant switch. Most of all, this experience of deprivation changed his outlook on life, mostly because he was able to forget the difficult parts and concentrate instead on the things that he most valued.

Nobody knew who I was there so I tried to be different, more like I really wanted to be. I started over. Sometimes I think about how I was there. I think about the fun times. I think about the new things I tried—bungy jumping, caving, having sisters for the first time. I don't really think much about how lonely I felt, or scared sometimes, or how mean some kids were to me. I'd lay in bed at night and think about everyone and everything I miss. I had to be an optimist. I'd never, ever wish I hadn't done it. I just wish that it didn't have to be so hard.

What is it that happens when you travel like an anthropologist, forcing yourself to experience local customs, interacting with people in authentic ways, and diving into the culture with eager enthusiasm? Changes are evident on several levels.

Self-Identity

You learn to see yourself through others' eyes. It is not uncommon for people to find a new part of their own identity—as an American, a Catholic, a blonde, or as arrogant or passive—as a result of how others see them.

One woman explained to several other professional men who joined me in a discussion about what happens to them when they are traveling: "I don't associate what I do with who I am. I identify myself according to my relationships rather than my job." The men were puzzled, or course, so she elaborated further: "I don't lose a part of myself, or my identity, when I travel. I add to myself another layer."

It is only after we let go of the normal ways we define our identities—as parents and children, Canadians or Irish Americans, or Episcopalians or lawyers—that we are able to find a deeper, more essential part of who we are.

Self-Awareness

As a result of being subjected to new challenges and situations, you learn things about yourself in the process—what matters and what does not, what you can handle deftly and what you struggle with, what you avoid and what you gravitate toward, and what you miss most from back home and what you do not think about at all. Sometimes, as one person explains, it is painful to realize that you are not nearly as important as you think:

We all think we are indispensable. Nobody can ever do as good a job as you can. Rubbish! I went away for a month, traveling in the most exotic of locales, and the whole time I kept wondering about how things were going at work. How would they handle things while I was away? Would they miss me? Would things fall apart without me there to maintain control?

Boy, was I in for a surprise! When I came back, I found that I was hardly missed. Oh, my friends were quick to reassure me that they were glad I returned but it was obvious they'd all done fine without me. I realized, then and there, that I'm not nearly as important as I think I am.

Reflective Attitudes

Travel forces you to be more tolerant, more flexible, and more willing to deal with ambiguous circumstances. You question things more—for example, why you have always done things a particular way—and thereby consider other options. A traveler who returned from a transformative trip related the following to me:

Traveling taught me what a flyspeck my world is. I hear people complaining about their misery, yet when you see people's lives in India you can't help but shake your head at them. Getting far enough away from what I'm used to helped me gain perspective on what's really important. What matters most are family and friends. I guess I knew that, but I didn't know that in my heart.

Self-Esteem

Any experience that forces you to cope in new ways, to solve problems and take care of yourself, results in increased self-esteem, especially if you feel successful in your efforts.

Carolee Taipale, the director of international programs at a small college in the Midwest, talks with hundreds of students about their travels abroad. By far the most frequent comments she hears from those who have returned from trips is that they feel a tremendous surge of confidence, like they can do anything after having survived all the usual mishaps and disasters that befall the traveler. Second, she notes that the students who have spent time abroad are more flexible than those who stay close to home.

Sometimes, the differences on returning home are quite profound, resulting in major personality transformations. The following is an example that Taipale describes from the cases she has supervised:

One woman went to Australia for a semester. Before she left, nothing ever seemed to go right for her. She came across as negative, a whiner, a complainer. She never seemed to smile. She was not a pleasant person to be around.

She returned to campus one of the most upbeat, smiling, joking, happy people you would ever want to meet. Sure, she had some complaints about her trip, but she turned them into positive experiences. She was unable to purchase a plane pass while she was in Australia so she was stuck taking trains the full length of that gigantic place. She loved it! This trip turned her into an amazing person.

A number of studies have noted that travel not only changes attitudes and characteristics in the present but also alters people's plans for the future. They are no longer willing to settle for a level of mediocrity in relationships, job satisfaction, and lifestyle that they have tolerated throughout most of their lives.

For example, it was not until she was almost 40 years old that Angel began bicycling in a serious way. As she explained:

I saw this article in a magazine about a guy organizing a trip around the world. Two years to cover the globe by bike. I thought to myself that was crazy. Who could spend that kind of time traveling? Besides, I've never been particularly athletic. I'd never even ridden more than a dozen miles at any one time.

The more I thought about it, the more I felt drawn to the possibility. Before I knew it, I had quit my job, sold everything I could, and we were on the road.

At the 16th month of her adventure, Angel still had a fair bit of territory left to cover. Nevertheless, she had already learned so much about herself:

Mostly, I realized that although I'm not especially smart or strong, I can still reach the same place as anyone else . . . eventually. When we are all riding together, I'm always the last one in line. But I'm there in the end.

There started out being 20 of us; now there are 13 left. The ones who dropped out were a lot better cyclists than me. It takes something more than endurance and fitness and skill to do this. And whatever that is, I learned that I've got it!

I asked her what difference that would make to her when she got home. Angel began beaming. Her voice speeded up as she confided: "I'll never settle again for the kind of boring life I had before. I had never traveled much before this trip. Now there is nothing that will ever hold me back again."

Get Out and Walk

Traveling like an anthropologist models to our students that we are open to change and new experiences in the same ways that we wish for them. It demonstrates our courage to face the unknown and to give up what is most familiar in pursuit of novel experiences.

Such change is more likely to take place when you venture into new territory rather than visiting somewhere you have been before. John Morris (1943), an Englishman living in Japan, found the perfect cone of Mount Fuji to be among the most spectacular sights on earth. Again and again, he would view the peak at dawn, reveling in its symmetry and simplicity. Once he decided to climb the mountain, its magic was destroyed forever. Litter was scattered along the trail everywhere. By the time he reached the summit, Morris was in the company of a thousand other hikers who had the same idea. One of his Japanese friends remarked to him that Fuji was a "seeing" mountain rather than a "climbing" one. Morris stated, "The Japanese, however, have a saying that there are two kinds of fool: those who have never climbed Mount Fuji, and those who have climbed it more than once."

It is one kind of sin to not sample as many Mount Fujis of the world as you can in a lifetime; it is quite another to return again to a place you have already visited when there are so many others waiting to be discovered. Transformative travel results when your core is shaken, when you interact personally and profoundly with the place and people you are visiting. To do that, you must leave the comfort of the tour bus. Better yet, get out and walk.

Machines, according to Robyn Davidson who writes about her adventures traveling across America on motorcycle, insulate us from change:

> When you ride a machine, you are always on your way to somewhere, you are never actually "there." When you walk, you are always "there" and can never get away from "there." It gives you time to ponder and be changed.

If walking helps you to interact more intimately with your surroundings, then so does getting outside the homogenized, insulated world of tourist hotels. You will never know what life is really like in the places you visit if you stay only in hotels and eat exclusively in restaurants. The object is to avoid places that are designed to provide familiar environments to tourists and business travelers who want only what they are used to getting. It is by viewing things from the inside that you can truly get a taste for the unique habits and customs of people in particular areas. This can only help you once you return home and face the usual challenges that are part of your classroom.

In Table 6.1, I offer reflective questions as a structure by which you might consider writing, or at least thinking, about what you would like to have happen as a result of a particular trip. After you return, it is also important to consider the extent to which you have made the changes you were looking for. Like so many learning experiences, whether in a course, lecture, workshop, or trip, effects do not often last very long unless you make concerted efforts to maintain the momentum.

It is not enough to observe something powerful nor even to talk about new insights you have had. You must also act in new ways. Therapists and teachers often construct experiences in session, or assignments outside of the classroom, that are conducive to (a) promoting enlightenment, (b) altering perceptions, and (c) stimulating new behaviors. The same is true with travel experiences that are most influential. Most likely, you have not only felt or thought in new ways but also behaved differently. Educational psychologists call this *direct experience,* referring to the kinds of "hands-on" activities that most reliably encourage people to change in lasting ways.

Table 6.1

Before	After
What aspect of your life would you most like to change?	What difference has the experience made?
What are you most afraid of?	How did you deal with your fears?
What are you searching for that this experience will provide?	What did you learn about yourself that you did not know?
What is it that attracts you to this particular activity?	What didn't you like about the experience?
How will you focus your attention on the present moment of what happens?	How can you create similar feelings in your daily life?
What is going on in your life right now that makes you ripe for this?	What do you resolve to do to apply what you learned?
What could you do instead of this that might accomplish the same thing?	Where will you look next to push yourself to the next level?

Cultural Lessons for the Teacher

It is neither practical nor realistic to expect that every teacher has the time, resources, or opportunity to live or work abroad, or even the inclination to travel extensively. Such far-flung adventures are not even necessary to reap benefits from expanding your cultural horizons through immersion in "foreign" places.

Certainly, there are a number of options available for the teacher who would like to spend extended time abroad. For the beginning teacher, it is easier than one might think to arrange student teaching assignments in other countries. For the veteran, options abound that include summer sabbaticals, job switching, or teaching in American schools abroad.

The point, however, is that it is not necessary to leave your continent, or even your own community, to experience significant cultural lessons. What going to another country, or even to a strange city, does is force us to give up the cultural referents that we are used to because they no longer work very well in a different context. As the following story demonstrates, our orderly routines that we think are so wonderful are not only inappropriate in other cultures but also spectacularly ineffective.

Constantine, who had been teaching for some years in a middle-class neighborhood school, had been feeling increasingly distressed and unprepared to deal with rapid changes in the cultural composition of his classroom. A number of immigrants from Asia and Latin America, as well as an influx of African American children, were creating a rich mix of cultures that was beyond his experience. Although these new children still represented a decided minority in the school, Constantine could see that this wave of diversity would only grow more pronounced in the future.

Constantine thought it might be a good idea to prepare himself better for the directions his school was headed, at least in terms of student population. He first contacted his principal to see if it might be possible to arrange for him to be placed in a more culturally diverse school for a semester or an academic year, especially one with a high concentration of Hispanic and African American students. What he had in mind was doing a kind of mid-career student teaching assignment.

Although his principal thought this was an intriguing idea, he listed a number of reasons why he did not think this plan could work. The school district would never go for it, in his considered opinion, but he nevertheless gave Constantine permission to pursue the matter. With persistence and a major investment of time, he was able to find a friend teaching the same schedule in another school across town who agreed to do a teacher exchange for a semester. Remarkably, he even got the two principals and the district to approve the project.

Little did he realize that the hardest work of all would begin once he began his immersion in a different culture. Constantine was by no means an inexperienced teacher. In fact, he considered himself one of the most highly skilled and dedicated teachers in his school (this is certainly not surprising given his motivation to undertake this project in the first place). Nevertheless, he found that working in his new classroom was like beginning anew; it was like being a student teacher again.

Lesson plans that had served him well for years failed miserably with his new group of students. Discipline strategies that he thought were foolproof turned out to be utterly useless in his new environment. Even his jokes fell flat.

Constantine found that before he could ever hope to reach these children, he would first have to know them. They seemed so different, however. He could not make sense of their behavior at times, and he could not even begin to understand why they were acting in particular ways and why they did not seem to care much for things that other children seemed to value.

It was a humbling experience for Constantine. In all fairness, in a single semester, he did not function or feel very effective. He did, however, make light-years of progress in expanding his repertoire of cultural understanding and responsiveness. What surprised him most was that when he returned to his old school, people there considered him to be the expert on cultural diversity, even with only a few months experience. Nevertheless, he did learn far more about teaching in that semester than he had in any previous block of time he could remember since student teaching a decade earlier.

Within the Borders of Your Community

There are many other ways that teachers can live and teach as anthropologists without having to leave the borders of their nation or town. Being a teacher gives us a license to knock on the doors of schools anywhere in the world. You will be amazed at how warmly you will be welcomed.

For example, while in Kuching, Borneo, a few years ago, I was walking around some back streets when I stumbled on the sounds of children playing. Following the noise, I found myself standing in front of the gates of Kuching High School. Before I lost my nerve, I strode in through the entrance and introduced myself to the principal as a visiting teacher who was interested in learning about what they were doing in their school. I was amazed at how delighted he was to show me around the school and to let me visit some classrooms. Before I knew it, they turned over an English class to me for the period to talk with the children and let them practice their language skills. What an adventure! All it took was the courage to enter through the gates.

Since then, I have made a point to visit a school in whatever city I am visiting, whether it is on the other side of the world or in a neighboring community. I know that the only way I can truly stretch myself as a teacher is by finding out as much as I can about how other colleagues, who operate under different circumstances, work their magic with children.

It is not enough to visit a school or simply take a trip that produces tremendous growth. Rather, it is thinking like an anthropologist that helps us to increase our awareness of different cultures. It is through such visits that we are able to open our minds to new possibilities and release our imaginations to consider creative alternatives (Jantz & Weaver, 1992). This expanded vision of what is possible in education with people of different experiences and backgrounds is what keeps us fully engaged in the process of teaching as an adventure rather than as merely a job.

Part II

Purposeful Actions

Being and Doing Things Differently in the Classroom

Jeffrey A. Kottler
and
Ellen Kottler

Too often in our education, inservice workshops, journal articles, books, and motivational speeches, we hear about innovative and creative ways to make our classrooms more multicultural in emphasis. We are hungry for new techniques and lesson plans. We love specific ideas that we can immediately convert into more engaging bulletin boards or class sessions. The more concrete the better.

Although doing things differently in the classroom is certainly important if we are to have any lasting impact on an increasingly diverse student population, a few minor additions to our pedagogical bag of tricks is just not going to do the job we have in mind.

Being Rather Than Doing

The problem with supposedly "foolproof" methods is that we get the distinct impression from their authors that if, for some reason, the methods do not work, it is our fault. Time after time, we have come home from a particularly inspiring presentation determined that we will employ some of the innovative methods that were introduced. When we apply these techniques in our own classrooms, however, they often do not have quite the same effects as we were promised. Part of the reason is certainly related to our inexperience with new skills and ways of thinking, but the other part has to do with the phenomenon that people rarely talk about their mistakes and failures. When was the last time you attended a workshop or in-service program when the presenters regaled you with stories, or showed videotapes, in which they made absolute fools of themselves? When was the last time you read accounts in which authors who were selling a particular ideology or methodology presented cases in which their favored strategies failed miserably?

Another problem is that, very often, techniques are based on the assumption that they can be universally applied to all children in any circumstances. Ballenger (1992) describes how she learned this lesson well when working with Haitian children in a preschool. She found herself unable to control her class, even with her most time-tested strategies that had been drilled into her from her teacher training. Still, the kids ran her ragged.

Interestingly, however, the Haitian teachers in the same school did not encounter these problems. As much as she wanted to blame the kids, or her flawed methods, eventually she had to acknowledge that perhaps she was the problem.

After reflecting not so much on what she was doing, but rather on how she was "being" in the presence of the children, Ballenger (1992) concluded that she would have to make some major changes in her own attitudes and outlook if she was ever to be successful with her students. She received the following feedback and advice from her Haitian colleagues:

1. Stop commenting and reflecting on student feelings (e.g., "You're angry at her for pushing you") because this is not appropriate in Haitian culture.

2. Rather than finding causes to explain why children are mis-behaving, it is far more effective to focus on group responsi-bility (e.g., "We don't act like that here").
3. Do not make immediate consequences explicit (e.g., "You'll miss recess if you don't stop"). Instead, talk generally about how all bad behavior brings shame to one's family.
4. Whenever possible, use rhetorical questions with "no" answers—for example, "Did I tell you to leave your seat?" "No." "Why do I want you remain there?" "Because you like us."

What all these add up to is not a prescriptive formula for teaching Haitian children, although these suggestions would certainly prove useful as a guide. Most of what Ballenger (1992) mentions violates everything she ever learned in teacher training. We have been taught to avoid such methods as verbal rebukes, close-ended questions, and shaming children. These are precisely the strategies that young Hai-tian students responded to best, however.

Within mainstream North American culture, and certainly most teacher education programs, we emphasize individualism and self-responsibility again and again. Prominent among our most cherished assumptions is the idea that when a child acts poorly it is because of something lacking in that individual—a streak of laziness, a weak character, or perhaps a mischievous spirit. As such, the things we do in the classroom to fix these maladies are intended to make children more self-controlled, self-responsible, and self-sufficient. Obviously, *self* is the operative word.

The problem, however, lies in the fact that for many children who originate from Asia, Latin America, and the Third World, shared values and responsibility to the family and community are consid-ered far more important than self-oriented needs. This means that teachers would not only have to act differently in how they teach and manage behavior but also have to be different in the style with which they respond to children.

How are we ever expected to know the unique requirements for each child—not only for Haitians but also for Hmung, Vietnamese, Sri Lankans, Ogala Sioux, Bolivians, or any of the dozens of other cultural groups represented in our classes? The answer is found in our own openness and willingness to learn as much as we can about cultural differences as well as to develop a flexible way of being that allows us to make cultural adjustments when things do not work out as expected. When you try explaining consequences to a child with no visible effect, it is time to reflect on your behavior as well as that of the student who appears resistant. Such conflicts in the classroom are just as often the result of the teacher's rigidity or ignorance as they are the student's attitude (Kottler, 1997a).

Truly transformative learning takes place within a particular cultural context, one in which there is a pervasive atmosphere of respectful curiosity and tolerance. This can take place only when we, as teachers, have been able to create a classroom culture that is embracing enough to help students of all backgrounds feel welcome. This does not happen with a few clever interventions or dynamite activities. The "doing" follows being.

In other words, although we talk about different things that teachers can do to make their classrooms more inviting and stimulating, we acknowledge that these efforts are largely superficial unless embedded in a philosophy, or more descriptively as "a way of being," in which the teacher projects the very spirit of a human and humane model.

What does such a person look like? How does such a teacher behave? These questions are easier to answer than you might at first suppose. You would only have to look at your own best experiences in a student role. First of all, you would hardly nominate the best teacher you ever had as one who introduced a single teaching method that bowled you over. Rather, day in and day out in this class you were supported, provoked, and challenged. Furthermore, the growth you experienced certainly did not result from one thing the teacher did but rather from a thousand different actions that were all variations of a single theme.

This teacher you have in mind, the one who influenced you the most, did a number of things that appear to be fairly universal in people's reports on teaching excellence (Zehm & Kottler, 1994). Most of all, he or she was caring and charismatic.

If our intent is to truly make a difference in the lives of students who need help the most, we must change the usual ways we go about our business. It is because of the various cultures within each student that unique learning styles and sources of motivation must be identified and responses must be developed. This requires a degree of flexibility, adaptability, and creativity that is, at once, quite challenging and exhilarating.

Work Within the Student's Culture

A student's behavior does not occur in isolation. It is cued by what you are doing, by what others are doing both inside the class and inside the school, as well as by the larger community.

Children sometimes act out because they are "designated" to do so by other members of their culture. For example, as long as Trent causes problems in school, he is a convenient distraction for his parents so they can avoid dealing with their crumbling marriage. Once the phone calls from you stop, signaling that Trent is now doing well in school, his parents start fighting again. They stop only when it is required for them to come together to help their child. Naturally, you are going to have a very difficult time getting through to Trent unless you can understand the larger picture of how his behavior is being triggered by others without his awareness.

Sometimes, these kinds of cultural influences are very subtle. Unless you can establish the kind of relationship with the child in which he or she will tell you the background that you need to understand what is going on, your job will be much harder. For example, Kim is a first-generation Cambodian immigrant who came to North America with her mother. The two of them were the only survivors of brutal atrocities committed against their large family by their own people and by American soldiers.

Kim had been one of the best students in class—cooperative, polite, but with a spark of passion. Seemingly without warning, she became morose and withdrawn. In response to invitations to participate in class, she would act surly and unresponsive.

Eventually, through much patience and compassion, the teacher learned that Kim had lately been doing some reading about her heritage and homeland and how her country had been raped and its people subjected to numerous atrocities. It was especially disturbing to hear stories from her mother of how her other children (Kim's siblings) had been unceremoniously killed by American soldiers before her mother's very eyes.

Kim now viewed her adopted country with ambivalence. Authority figures such as teachers became the target of her resentment. This was not necessarily a rational connection, but nevertheless one that somehow made sense to her. It was only by hearing her story, and learning about Kim's cultural background, that the teacher was able to get a handle on the changes that had been taking place. This became the beginning for them to reforge a relationship.

In all the methods and suggestions presented throughout this and other chapters, it is understood that they will take place within a particular relationship with students: One that is respectful and caring. Because it is likely that whenever you are experimenting with new strategies you are likely to make mistakes and feel awkward during the process, you will need the indulgence and forgiveness of your students when things do not develop as expected and preferred. Within the context of a solid relationship, it is not very difficult to admit, "Oh well. I guess that didn't work out very well, did it? Let's try something else."

Learning the Rules
Within Student Cultures

One of the first things that teachers can do differently is to see the value of cultural sensitivity in their teaching methods. One mathematics teacher, speaking for a large number of colleagues, complains, "Multicultural education is bunk. An equation is an equation. It doesn't matter who you are teaching. The content is the same."

Another point against overattention to cultural differences is presented by Ogbu (1992, p. 6), who stated that "multicultural education generally ignores the minority students' own responsibility for their academic performance." Indeed, to a certain extent, teachers are responsible for student learning. What about the students' own role in furthering their progress? Shouldn't they be responsible for translating concepts and ideas into terms that fit best their own needs?

Ogbu (1992) mentions that is it helpful for teachers to understand some of the differences between various cultures, dividing them into distinct groups. The first group, "autonomous minorities," is composed of cultures such as Jews, Mormons, and Amish. The second group, "immigrant or voluntary minorities," consists of cultures such as the Chinese and Punjabi Indians. These people chose to come to North America and may initially have problems due to cultural and language differences. They see learning as useful and hope it will help them toward economic achievement. They expect to learn the ways of the new culture. They work hard to overcome problems. They do whatever is necessary to succeed.

The third group, "caste-like or involuntary minorities," consists of people who were forced against their will into their current circumstances. This includes groups such as African Americans, American Indians, and early Mexican Americans. This group has the greatest difficulty adjusting to school and displays cultural patterns that are different from those of the mainstream society even though members of this group develop secondary cultural differences, especially those that involve the domination of one group by another. This group evolves particular styles of communication, interaction, and learning.

Another feature of the involuntary minority group members that is very obvious in schools today is the attitude of "cultural inversion"—that it is okay for their behaviors to be different, or even opposite from sanctioned norms, because they are not part of the mainstream. Perhaps the best examples of this are the frequent tardiness to class and the nature of loud, often X-rated communication of students.

There is no reason or payoff for these students to give up their ways because they would lose their identity. The students may not even be aware of their contributions in building or maintaining the walls that prevent them from succeeding. They do not see many models who have crossed the barriers successfully and who are fully accepted by whites.

One teacher describes her observations related to this phenomenon as follows: "I have one black, teenage female student for two classes during the day. In the first class, she walks with another black friend to class, always late. In the second class, though, she comes by herself, always on time."

The voluntary minority members do not need the same type of help as the involuntary minority members. The voluntary minority members strive for good grades and have the social support they need from their families and communities. The involuntary minority members, however, need special methods to help them succeed.

Whereas some students develop strategies on their own, there are several things teachers can do to facilitate the process.

First of all, teachers can learn about the histories and adaptations of the groups of students in their classes to understand their behavioral patterns. Bintz (1995) speaks about his efforts to learn from his students what they know, what they value, and what they believe in: "In my experience, when inclusivity was highlighted and voice was supported, I was able to hear how different students described and named their cultural world" (p. 41). This meant learning about their unique customs, their traditional foods, and their favored myths and stories. Most of all, it meant that he was changed in the process: "I have come to believe that schooling is an opportunity for teachers and students to see, hear, and think differently about themselves and about each other as learners" (p. 42).

Making Learning Culturally Relevant

Although a veteran history teacher of 20 years, Harris (1995) describes her rebirth as a multicultural teacher, one who is now learning and relearning the subject she has supposedly been an expert in. She has filled gaps in her knowledge, exposed herself to multiple perspectives of the same events, altered her language when describing stories, and generally tried to involve students in the process by which history is created. Not merely satisfied with upgrading content, Harris has found that her teaching methods have also become invigorated by her multicultural investigations. She is no longer interested in teaching about history but rather in helping students to think critically about issues that matter most to them.

Banks (1995) urges teachers to help students integrate the personal knowledge of their cultures in their formal studies: When did your ancestors arrive in America? What was life like for them? What were their struggles? Their accomplishments? What family stories do you have? What family records do you have?

Banks (1991) illustrates several kinds of knowledge that can be included in addition to traditional, mainstream thought. These include personal and cultural contributions from each student's history; popular knowledge from movies, television, and the media; transformative academic perspectives that challenge mainstream thought; and school facts presented by teachers and resource materials. The goal of all this is to help students understand how everything they learn is constructed within a social context—one that they can be a part of building. This constructivist approach gives students the responsibility for their own knowledge. The role of the teacher is to structure a democratic classroom in which students can discuss and evaluate varied points of view.

Timm (1996) categorizes these ideas into three areas of knowledge for multicultural education—cultural information that she refers to as (a) curricular content, such as history, biographies, values, art, science, literature, technology, and material and nonmaterial culture; (b) social issues aimed at combating biases, such as attitudes of ageism, ethnocentrism, prejudice, racism, sexism, and stereotypes; and (c) interrelationships or behavioral processes including, but not limited to, relationships between home and school, student to student, and teacher to student, and self-esteem, learning styles, and ethics of care.

With regard to each of the three areas, there are different factors for consideration. With respect to cultural information, teachers need to plan for the developmental level of the classroom, the accuracy of the material, and any biases reflected in the material.

Some Things You Can Do

Although the following chapters will provide in greater detail some approaches for making classrooms more culturally sensitive and invigorated, here a mere sampling of things you can do is provided. Our intent is not to provide an exhaustive list but rather to tease your own imagination with possibilities. We further urge you to suspend your critical internal voice—that part of you that shakes your head in amusement as you list all the reasons why these methods are impractical or inappropriate. Just as you complain that your students will not take responsibility for adapting content to fit their own unique needs, we urge you to do the same.

- *Help even marginal students to feel competent.* In her study of teachers who are especially effective with African American children, Ladson-Billings (1994) observed that one important classroom principle is that everyone, even the outcasts, are helped to become intellectual leaders. All students are treated as if they are competent and already know something. The culture of the children is imported into the classroom so that all learning becomes connected to the realities of their everyday lives.

- *Involve students' families.* Many cultural groups to which students belong emphasize family involvement in all matters of importance. This is especially true in Latin and Asian cultures in which family values supersede individual preferences. Carger and Ayers (1995) recommend that parents and other family members be treated as valuable sources of knowledge not only about their child but also about their cultural heritage. They further urge educators to "irregularize" their rooms to accommodate the contributions of students' families, creating "dynamic, multifaceted and diverse communities of learners" (p. 6).
- *Recruit role models.* Invite prominent people from the community who are representatives of the cultural groups in your class to visit your students and speak about their successes. In one third-grade class that was composed principally of African American youngsters, the white teacher increased her own credibility in the eyes of her students by inviting quite a number of African American leaders to come to the class. The kids were not only proud of the contributions of these men and women but also impressed that their teacher was so well connected that she could persuade these busy people to visit.
- *Structure diverse cooperative learning groups.* All the advantages of self-directed student groups described by Slavin (1990) are heightened further when members of various cultural groups are required to work together cooperatively to accomplish mutually satisfying goals, especially when there are group rewards and individual accountability. A dramatic example of the power that selective matching can have is illustrated by a physical education teacher who was working with a group of at-risk children on a "ropes course" in an adventure-based model:

> There were these two guys in the group who hated each other's guts. They were constantly getting into it with each other, at each other's throats, and stirring up everyone else as well. You could just feel the tension with them glaring at each other all the time.

Finally, I'd had enough. I teamed them up together and told them they had to climb to the top of a tall tree using rungs on a rope ladder that became increasingly further apart as they progressed upward. Naturally, they started out very competitive and began racing one another to the top, even pushing each other down as they climbed higher. Finally, they got to the point where they could go no higher without the cooperation of the other boy to push or pull each of them to the next level. To make things even tougher, they were by now high enough that the view was quite frightening, and the ropes began twisting and twirling from their combined weight. They had to help one another or they would both be humiliated in front of their friends.

By the time the boys came down they were both white in the face. Even more compelling, though, was the way their attitude changed to one another. After that, they each felt a grudging respect for one another.

- *Use games whenever possible.* Similar to cooperative learning, when students are placed in teams they become members of the same group and must work together to meet a challenge. They develop friendships at the same time. There are games that can be used in the academic area of the teacher's choice, from math and science to history and foreign language.
- *Invite students to research and teach their worldview.* Regardless of what you are teaching, there are multiple cultural views of how the content should be applied, what its relative importance is when compared to other issues, and even divergent views on what things mean. Invite students to personalize material by giving them assignments to find out what their familial and cultural perspectives are on the subject. Then give them opportunities to teach others about what they discovered, always in a spirit of respect for differences.
- *Bring gender differences into prominence.* Encourage students to appreciate and value how they feel, think, and respond to the world as a function of their gender roles. Help them to examine which gender values are most limiting and which are most constructive.

How children react emotionally to incidents in their lives is shaped, to a great extent, by the norms for their gender. When disappointed or frustrated, boys typically react in anger or aggression, whereas girls are more likely to express themselves verbally or through tears (Kottler, 1996). It is fascinating, therefore, to encourage children to expand their repertoire of choices when faced with struggles. Boys might be asked to talk about only how they feel about a matter, whereas girls would be encouraged to say only what they think.

- *Bring the subject of prejudice and racism into the classroom.* Allow children to talk about how they have suffered discrimination in their lives and what that felt like. Provide opportunities for children to examine social and historical realities.
- *Start with what the students know.* Constructivist approaches to teaching emphasize the importance of building on what students already know and understand. New units are introduced with questions or statements to encourage active participation. For example, a teacher might begin a social studies unit by asking, "What are some of the things you already know about why wars begin?" Further questions are then asked to establish a core knowledge base on which to build. This approach not only checks the entry level of students, and involves them directly at the beginning of the lesson, but also incorporates the diversity of experiences represented in class.
- *Relate material to a cultural context.* When teaching any unit, steer away from presenting "objective reality" and instead introduce ideas of cultural relevance—that all knowledge exists in a particular context. For example, when teaching handwriting to early elementary-age children, explore other forms of written communication and how some samples have endured for centuries because they were comprehensible and legible. Also introduce the traditions of oral historical records through stories, songs, and dance. Encourage children to research the traditional methods of passing on knowledge in their own culture.
- *Emphasize the dignity and pride of being members of various cultures.* Children's portraits (either Polaroid photos or self-drawings) can be displayed, showing their dominant cultural heritages through images, symbols, or words.
- *Inventory and assess communication styles.* Ask yourself whether there are any problems in the classroom due to miscommunication. Students from various backgrounds differ in their verbal communication patterns, including the tempo of speech and words they

stress; nonverbal communication such as avoiding eye contact as a sign of respect; proxemics—the comfortable distance between two people; interpersonal touching—for example, a light pat rather than a firm touch on the shoulder; and intellectual orientations— some cultures value questioning, whereas others discourage it. Some students will nod their heads in the affirmative to be polite rather than indicate that they do not understand a question or have not completed an assignment. Other students expect specific directions before carrying out a task and therefore may not show initiative in selecting learning activities or working on their own.

- Use technology. As will be described in Chapter 9, technology can be used to help students increase their awareness of other cultures around the world as well as to connect with members of their own culture. With the increasing use of computers in the classroom, electronic mail helps students to work on collaborative projects with others around the world, to collect information of interest, and to develop relationships with others from other countries.

- Reach out to non-native English speakers. If you have limited- or non-English-proficient speakers, there are several strategies that you can employ to make life easier for them (E. Kottler, 1994). First, when speaking, use as many concrete examples as possible with actual objects, props, or visual aids. Target your own vocabulary, identifying which words are central to understanding. Make sure everyone knows the meaning of your words before you begin your lesson. Provide a dictionary of those terms that are central to the lesson for the English language learner. This could be a list of words with pictures or definitions in the native language or simple definitions in English. Another strategy that is not nearly as time-consuming is to provide an outline for them to follow.

    Be cognizant of your own language. Idioms can be a great challenge. Abbreviations can be frustrating. Watch out for puzzled looks when you use homonyms—words that have the same pronunciation but different spelling. You might pronounce words differently, which may cause some confusion.

Each of these suggestions that you can do in your classroom to make things more culturally sensitive and responsive can spawn another dozen ideas of your own. The specifics of what you do are less important than the overriding attitude that you show, communicating that you are interested in your students' cultural backgrounds, that you value their differences, and that you intend to do all within your power to make your classroom safe for a free exchange of ideas in which everyone is respected and valued.

In the chapters that follow, the authors introduce several practical ways that you can translate the ideals of multicultural education into action-oriented ways of thinking and acting. In the narrative approach in Chapter 8, a constructionist model is adapted from the arena of counseling to make classrooms more stimulating.

Narrative Approaches to Culture and Learning

Gerald Monk

and

Jeffrey A. Kottler

Jeremy was the center of attention in the teachers' lounge, although he did not know it. Jeremy's teacher, Diana, was sitting with three of her colleagues talking about her frustrations in dealing with this child who she could not control. In fact, she could not think of a time she felt more discouraged.

Diana said with a deep sigh:

I can't believe how out of control this kid is. He rarely sits in his chair and is more likely to be flitting around the room getting into other children's stuff. He can't concentrate on anything. He can't stay with one project for more than a minute. He's really excitable. Honestly, I don't know what to do with him. He's driving me crazy!

Diana was an enthusiastic third-year history teacher, among the most popular in her New Zealand school. She generally kept 13-year-old students busy in her classes with exciting projects. For example, they had just completed a map-making exercise of the *pa* sites (a pa is a traditional fortified village built by the indigenous people of New Zealand, the Maori, prior to the arrival of European settlers in the late 18th century).

Despite how interesting a task might be, Jeremy could stay focused for only a few minutes at the most. He would initially show some interest, even some satisfaction in the project, and then he would walk around the classroom annoying his peers and his teacher.

A number of different suggestions surfaced in the teachers' lounge about what to do with Jeremy. Pauline, one of the more experienced teachers in the school, believed that Jeremy had some kind of attention deficit disorder. She therefore suggested that Jeremy's parents should be consulted and arrangements made for him to be placed on medication to control his symptoms.

Josephine, another experienced teacher listening in on the conversation, considered herself to be an expert in behavior modification strategies. She suggested that it was a better idea to put Jeremy on some kind of behavioral contract in preference to medicating him. She proposed that Diana needed to set some very specific goals with Jeremy about appropriate academic and social behavior. Diana needed to work out with him what reinforcers could be applied to reward him for on-task behavior and what consequences could be introduced to shape appropriate classroom behavior.

Donna, the third teacher who had been part of the discussion, had been on the staff of this junior high school for many years. She knew many of the families in the valley, as well as a little about Jeremy's background, because she was actively involved in the local Maori community. She revealed that he did not live with his parents because they had been killed in a car accident 3 years previously. Now, he was living with his uncle and aunt. She also recalled that his grandfather had died 3 weeks ago and she had been to the *tangi*,[1] a communal funeral, although she had not seen Jeremy there—an unusual occurrence in any traditional Maori community.

Donna suggested to Diana that Jeremy may be very distressed about not being able to attend this important ceremony for his grandfather. She wondered further whether it was Jeremy's grief that had contributed to his out of control behavior because he had not always been this easily distracted.

Diana was flooded with possibilities. Was this behavior related to a psychological disorder that required medical treatment? Were there specific teaching strategies she should put in place to attend to his social, behavioral, and learning difficulties? Was Jeremy's disruptive behavior related to grieving and loss of his grandfather and perhaps his parents? How could Jeremy's problems be understood?

To complicate the matter further, Diana is of European background, whereas Jeremy is of Maori ancestry. Their respective peoples have a long history of conflict, mistrust, and mutual resentment. How will their cultural differences be managed?

If Diana takes Pauline's advice, she will be directed to a biochemical solution to her difficulties with Jeremy. The people that advocate this orientation would see the source of the difficulties resulting from some form of disruption in Jeremy's neurological system. Cultural differences will be considered peripheral in these circumstances.

The behavioral strategies suggested by Josephine are based on scientific principles utilized by the same modernistic tradition that inspires medical research. Knowledge acquired through the study of rats and pigeons has been applied to human behavior. From this orientation, Jeremy's problems are seen to emerge from behavioral consequences that reinforce his out-of-seat, running-around-the-room behaviors. The belief is that if the events occurring both immediately before and after his inappropriate classroom behavior were to change, his behavior could be altered to a more preferred direction. Again, the emphasis is on the application of expert technology that looks at culture to the extent that only the discriminative stimuli and subsequent consequences feature cultural content.

Although a medical or behavioral intervention may be a valid choice in working with Jeremy, in this chapter we introduce another perspective that is particularly well suited to examining behavior in its cultural context.

Narrative Approach

A narrative approach to education is one in which all life, and therefore all learning, is understood as a constructed story that gives coherence, order, and meaning to events, providing both a past and a future for present experience (Rappaport, 1993). What this means is that teachers must begin by understanding what stories their children live by. This has the following distinct advantages:

1. All people, and all children in particular, are used to thinking in terms of stories.
2. The construction of stories is an active process not only for the author but also for the listener.
3. There are an infinite number of interpretations possible for any story, allowing each child to insert a cultural context for what is heard.
4. Learning is based on direct experience in which the child is helped to create meaning from what was learned.

In this chapter, a narrative approach to working with the issues that have arisen between Diana and Jeremy is introduced. In addition, how the distinct child and adult cultures contribute to their misunderstanding is examined. Compatible with constructivist theory, which is becoming increasingly popular in education, the use of narrative approaches to learning is focused on how knowledge is created by the individual. For example, how is Jeremy understanding what is currently happening to him? What is his experience like of losing his parents 3 years earlier? How is he experiencing the recent loss of his grandfather? What does it mean to him that he was not able to participate in the *tangi?* What does it mean for him to be Maori in a classroom of people who have white-colored skin? These questions will be returned to at the end of the chapter.

Before exploring the use of narrative approaches for working with Jeremy, an overview of some of the theory and techniques associated with narrative approaches to teaching is presented. In doing so, constructivist theory, the learning environment, and adult and child cultures are discussed. Then, some aspects of narrative approaches to teaching are discussed, including narrative questioning, the use of externalizing, relative influence questions, the significance of the story metaphor, and some of the accompanying practices that are central to their successful implementation.

Brief Review of Constructivist Theory

There is a great deal of literature and research available about the significance of teachers' understanding of the cultural world of the children they teach (Biggs & Moor, 1993; Cornbleth, 1990; Lefrancois, 1991; McGuiness & Nisbet, 1991; Snook, 1992; Von Glaserfeld, 1990; Wittrock, 1977). Throughout *What's Really Said in the Teachers' Lounge*, a number of perspectives have been presented, most of which bear at least some resemblance to what could be called a constructivist approach.

Although constructivism is one of those politically correct ideas that is currently making the rounds, there are some legitimate reasons for its current popularity, especially when examining cultural factors that affect education. The narrative approach to learning, in particular, is based on a brand of social construction that has emerged during the past two decades not only in North America but also in Australia and New Zealand.

Constructivist theory views learning as a generative process. The child does not receive knowledge passively through the senses or thoughts but rather knowledge is actively constructed and manufactured out of a variety of stimuli, experiences, and expectations. To construct new knowledge from incoming stimuli, the learner is reliant on what is already known to process this new information. Thus, from this theoretical standpoint, what can be learned is dependent on what is already known (Biggs & Moor, 1993; Snook, 1992). This may not seem like a very radical notion because most teachers would agree that to help someone learn something, they must know what the students already know. Unfortunately, we do not often practice this belief as much as we could. We do not take much time to find out what children already know—for example, how they construct their understanding of reading or geometry or shooting a basketball; often, we just jump in and begin the instruction without considering the variations in cultural interpretation.

This technocratic approach to learning has been the dominant curriculum development model during the past few decades

(Cornbleth, 1990). For example, Taba (1962) advocated a teaching model in which the teacher dictates, controls, and instructs. This orientation views the teacher as the deliverer of expert knowledge and regards the "customers" of this service as being on roughly equal footing. Of course, this model is at odds with the theory of the centrality of children's existing knowledge as the guide to new learning tasks in the classroom.

Consistent with a constructivist approach, using narrative approaches in the classroom invites the teacher to understand the learning process through the eyes of the student. The teacher is keenly interested in identifying how students approach a learning task and how their current knowledge draws on their individual, unique cultural filters.

Differences in Adult and Child Knowledge

In teacher training, many of us were taught to trust knowledge that is derived from a scientific method and distrust that which stems from other sources (intuition, spirituality, personal anecdotes, dreams, and fantasies). Most of all, we got the distinct impression that we, as adults, know what is best for children. It is our job, in fact, to tell them what they need to learn and then to make sure they learn it. Note, for example, the following comments reported by Mclean (1995) of two young people who had recently left school and who were now at different universities:

Annie: I think they really did think that we weren't to be trusted, and we didn't know what was good for us. And I think it would have been a lot better if we could have had some sort of influence over the way we were being treated, the way we were being taught and everything.

Emma: I hated the way the children were treated as if they really didn't have much of a brain at all. And I really hated the system. You always had to defer to a teacher as always being right, no matter what the situation was. You didn't have much of a leg to stand on if you wanted to dispute something a teacher had said or done. (pp. 43-44)

Although young people are often the objects of study, such as Jeremy's situation being discussed in the teachers' lounge, they are ordinarily precluded from speaking about their interpretations about their lives. This often leads to being excluded from examining their own motives reflected in their actions and being deprived of opportunities to review the consequences of their actions on themselves and on their relationships with others (White, 1995).

When teachers press students further, however, using some of the methods from narrative and other approaches, they often get surprising results. Try asking a student who says "I don't know" follow-up questions such as "If you did know, what would you say?" "Imagine there is a time in the future when you know the answer to that question. What might you say?" or "Take a wild guess, then what would the answer be?" We are often shocked, in such circumstances, that the problem is not that students do not know what they want, or even what they need, but rather that they are used to not feeling like their opinions really matter.

It is interesting that when attempts are made to measure what good teaching is, the attempts usually try to measure how much children improved on standardized tests or perhaps even examine the skill with which lectures are presented. We suggest, however, that another way to determine excellent teachers is to look at their use of expert questioning to uncover existing knowledge that children already possess.

To engage in a respectful exploration of the student's world, teachers first need to attend to the context in which they are working with their students. Jeremy's classroom environment will have an effect on the degree to which he is going to be open to sharing his own knowledge and understandings.

Application of
Narrative Approaches in the Classroom

For young people to voice their knowledge, views, and opinions, they must be in an environment that facilitates openness and in which they feel safe to express themselves honestly. For this atmosphere to be created, a number of factors must be considered.

Shared Ownership of the
Classroom Environment

Throughout the history of our profession, there have been debates regarding the relative importance of freedom versus control. Constructivists are hardly the first proponents to value the importance of freedom. In fact, when Hopkins (1994) describes a narrative approach to education he sounds very much like Carl Rogers and the humanists of the 1960s. Implicit in his approach are the assumptions that (a) students should be given as much freedom and responsibility as they can handle, (b) cooperative learning should be used rather than lectures, (c) portfolio assessments are preferred over objective tests, and (d) the teacher should act primarily as a consultant rather than as an instructor.

Indeed, like the "freethinkers" of the past, teachers using a narrative approach are sensitive to the kind of learning environment that they establish. For example, Diana had made special efforts to be sensitive to creating the kind of atmosphere in which the students felt like they belonged and had an opportunity to speak openly about their thoughts and views.

Narrative Questioning

Among all the contributions of the narrative approach is a unique form of questioning that we have adapted from therapeutic settings to those in the classroom. The object of this method is to discover, with the child, the particular meaning that learning has for him or her. This will then lead the child to higher levels of understanding, eventually resulting in changes in thinking and action.

Developing Trust and Safety

The successful use of narrative approaches to learning in the classroom is dependent on the creation of a positive relationship between teacher and student. For example, for Jeremy to feel sufficiently safe to share aspects of his internal world, a number of characteristics must be present. These include the kind of relationship in which the teacher really knows his or her students and their worlds (Fraser, 1994). We are speaking here about the distinctly human dimensions of teaching—those that communicate how much the teacher values and respects the students and trusts them to express what they really feel and think (Zehm & Kottler, 1994).

Effects of Culture on Child and Adult Interactions

A narrative approach to questioning requires the teacher to first view the students as possessing a body of knowledge about themselves and, when given an opportunity, they will bring this knowledge forward. Some children are very familiar with how to present their knowledge using adult constructions, and to do so reflects the children's wisdom and hard work to adjust themselves to the culture of the adult world. To do this well, however, a child must have a good working knowledge of the culture of the teacher to help the teacher make the information or knowledge fit with what the child is presenting. This means being good at knowing what teachers want to hear and how they want to hear it. If each of us were honest, we could list our very strong preferences for how we like students to be and the preferences we have for how they express themselves.

Young people such as Jeremy may be less familiar with the teacher's culture and are, therefore, at a disadvantage in being able to read correctly what is required to succeed. The student who does not know the teacher's culture will not be able to compete for attention and approval in the same way that other kids can. Knowing such things as how to raise your hand, to say "please" and "thank you," to maintain eye contact, and to be respectfully outspoken are just a few examples of the kinds of behavior that most of us prefer.

Critical theorists, such as Apple (1979), Cornbleth (1990), and Kemmis (1986), suggest that the classroom culture is controlled by certain sectors of society and, in particular, the middle class. Teachers, unaware of how they can contribute to reproducing dominant cultural knowledge, can unwittingly disadvantage many children or cause considerable distress to children who are not perceived to fit into the majority culture (whatever that may be).

Accessing Student Knowledge

The educator must work very hard to disrupt the tendency for young people to understand a phenomenon in black and white terms or as right or wrong. Although there are learning theories that suggest that children cannot search out the complexities and ambiguities in particular learning situations, it is also important to remember the strength of family, classroom, and the wider societal culture that encourages the children to divide things into simplistic categories of right and wrong and good and bad.

Questions are often shaped by the demands of adult culture that are not sensitive to the needs of a younger audience. Children may feel that their responses must be presented in a definitive and independent way. The "I don't know" answer is a sensible response made by young people who feel they do not have a definitive answer that will please and satisfy the adult questioner. This is in addition to the fact that the adult often wields considerable power over the children. The "I don't know" response maintains a degree of safety to protect them from potential humiliation. It is also acknowledged that a young person may genuinely have no way to produce an answer to a question that has little meaning to him or her. "I don't know" often means "I don't care."

We propose that much of a child's declared ignorance might actually relate to an inability as adults to develop the kinds of questions that might be expressed in an accessible way. In addition, the child conscious of the power differentials might be saying to himself or herself, "I do not have to tell you what I think and you can't make me" (White, 1995).

The teacher practicing a narrative approach first believes that the student possesses knowledge that, if given the opportunity to access it, will add considerably to the teaching of a subject or of assisting the child with his or her management of behavior. Students make their own best teachers.

Second, teachers must be passionately curious about the student's internal world and the knowledge and experiences that the student possesses. Teachers must engage with the student in the spirit of naivete about being interested in and fascinated with how the student understands a particular event or circumstance in his or her life. This is a position of "deliberate ignorance" in which teachers communicate that they really do not understand the world of the child but are intensely curious to be educated by the expert child in this domain.

Third, teachers must be respectfully persistent and creative in how they put forward a question. It is very easy to be put off by the well-used phrase "I don't know." In the following section, we explore how Donna began to implement some of new narrative learning into her interactions with Jeremy.

Jeremy's Story

By the end of the third week, Jeremy's behavior had deteriorated to the point that he was suspended from school for 3 days. He had cut a girl's hair and had pulled a boy's pants down. For him to return to school, a set of understandings had to be reached between the teacher and Jeremy and his family. Diana met with Jeremy and his aunt, during which time Jeremy had to produce a contract on the conditions that he thought he could meet and would be acceptable to the school. Diana asked Jeremy what he thought the problem was.

Jeremy replied that it had mainly to do with his classroom behavior, including racing around the room, upsetting people, and being disrespectful to the teachers. Jeremy said that he did want to come back to school and wanted to fit in more in class. They negotiated a contract that was quite a tough challenge for Jeremy, given how his behavior had been in recent times.

Diana was feeling out of her league and invited Donna, the Maori teacher, to assist her in working with Jeremy. Donna readily agreed. She was interested in trying some of the ideas she had gathered in a narrative approach to teaching conference she had participated in a few weeks before. She also wanted to work with Jeremy because he was one of the few Maori students in the school and one of the few brown-skinned children among a sea of white faces. Donna felt that she may have some things in common with Jeremy.

As with any culture, there are incredible complexities associated with being Maori, many of which would be foreign to not only most North Americans but also many New Zealanders. Donna's parents separated when she was 2 years old. Her father was Maori, but she had not had close contact with him during her school years. Her mother was Pakeha (white-skinned New Zealander). Although her skin pigment was brown, she had not believed herself to be Maori until she was 12 years old. At this stage, when many of the white-skinned children asked if she was Maori, she initially rejected this view because she saw herself like her mother. She was to discover, however, that her skin color had a significant impact on how she was treated in school. The Maori children initially did not accept her as one of them and the white-skinned children clearly saw her as Maori. Donna learned that the color of one's skin had real effects on how one was related to by other people. Donna felt that Jeremy was probably exposed to some racial prejudice because of his skin color, even though she knew very little about his upbringing and the significance that being Maori had for him.

The Dominant Story

All cultures generate stories to help people make sense of themselves and where they came from. Many of these stories originate from those created by our parents and caregivers or from some of our early experiences in school or at church or in any other significant environment in which we spend time during our formative years.

To make sense of the complexity of stimuli that come at us, we arrange information into a form that we can quickly make sense of. Often, this information is assembled in completed or fragmented story form. We develop dominant stories of our lives. We develop stories about whether we are an athletic person or a humorous person, whether we are academically bright, and whether we are bad or good, fun-loving or despondent, or attractive or ugly.

We "co-construct" these stories with those significant people who are in our lives. Once some of the dominant stories are constructed, we can more easily live in a way that attends to the contours of the stories that are laid before us. In other words, rather than living our lives first and then generating stories to describe our lives, it is the reverse that is true. The stories that are constructed about us are the ones that guide our behavior in the future. These stories have enormous implications for teachers working with their students. Jeremy's story was a good example of this phenomenon.

Donna asked Jeremy what he thought the problem was. He was very reluctant to speak at first. Slowly and hesitatingly he said that school was boring. Donna was very patient, warm, and encouraging. With persistence, she asked him why it was like this. He explained that he felt really dumb and did not think he would ever be able to learn in school.

During this interaction, Jeremy also told Donna that when he was little, his mother had taken him to a woman who had given him a number of tests and told them that he would never be able to learn in a conventional school because the teachers would not teach in a way that Jeremy needed to learn. He came to the conclusion that he was so unusual that the only way he could learn had not been figured out yet.

Jeremy had developed a story about his identity when he was very young and, to a large extent, arranged his life according to this early description. For many years, he had taken for granted that dumbness was the truth about him as a person. Jeremy believed that he was abnormal and could not learn with conventional methods, and it was confirmed by expert opinion.

In addition, Donna discovered that Jeremy had been preoccupied with the idea that he was also bad. With gentle curiosity, she discovered that Jeremy had felt that God was punishing him because of his badness. On what basis did he form that conclusion, Donna asked. That was obvious, he asserted. After all, hadn't everyone that he loved, or was close to, died? At this stage in Jeremy's life, he believed that the story of dumbness and badness had completely occupied his life as it rightly should because that was how life was.

From a narrative perspective, stories are viewed as making up our lives rather than the other way around. Many of the dominant stories match the dominant cultural attitudes that prevail in the community in which we participate. Teachers using narrative approaches are encouraged to see how the powerful cultural stories can shape many of the problems and difficulties that occur in the classroom. To a large extent, Jeremy did not feel that he fitted in at school. He was right: He was different in some pretty obvious ways.

Furthermore, Jeremy did not think his teachers knew anything about the kind of life he had, although he was now warming to Donna's attention and interest. Despite his personal turmoil, Jeremy was willing to give school another chance. He recognized that he needed to make some changes to stay in school.

Using Externalizations in Narrative Questioning

One of the techniques commonly associated with narrative approaches to helping and teaching uses the idea of "externalizing" problems (White & Epston, 1989). This occurs by talking about problems as external to the person rather than as part of that person's nature. Changing how problems are talked about opens up a language space to address the problem in a refreshingly different way while avoiding the stultifying effects of self-recrimination.

This technique presents a way of undermining a student's tendencies to internalize cultural messages that are located in the social context but understood to come from inside the person. For example, Jeremy's early evaluation that he was dumb and bad was a description that he located as coming from inside him. His conclusion about dumbness was based on the assumptions that (a) adults know better than children; (b) special tests can tell the truth about a person (adults believe that as well); and (c) when it is determined that you are not successful, it means you have some kind of deficit that needs to be fixed.

Obviously, Jeremy was not conforming to the dominant cultural attributes about what it means to be successful. In relation to his perceived "badness," he had been brought up in a religion that taught that people are divinely punished for their sins and, if forgiveness was not sought, some form of retribution was likely to follow. Therefore, it is not surprising that Jeremy came to these conclusions about himself as a bad person. He had carefully evaluated many aspects of his life to identify his sinful activity. His negative self-evaluation was not constructed separately from the culture that surrounded him while growing up. The cultures of the school, his church, and his ethnic background and social class have all played a significant role in producing the issues that were now prominent in his life. Like most people, Jeremy had not considered how the cultures surrounding him were the reference points used to produce this negative self-evaluation.

Jeremy had internalized the cultural messages and therefore had seen his difficulties as emerging from inside him. His negative self-assessment was based on some internal deficit that is often difficult to challenge and disrupt. Using externalizing principles, Jeremy's concerns could be seen to be constructed in the cultural milieu.

The use of externalizing conversations provides a vehicle to identify how the cultural messages construct the problem and give the teacher a structure to explore the role these messages play in producing problems.

In Donna's talk with Jeremy, she used the terms *dumbness* and *badness* to give focus to one of the major difficulties that was undermining Jeremy's attempts to create a life that gave him more favored options than the limited range of options he could currently choose from.

Relative Influence Questions

Relative influence questioning is used to explore the impact of the problem on the student and, conversely, to explore the impact the student has on the problem. When exploring the person's impact on the problem, this can be used to access the local or indigenous knowledge of the student in a particular problem domain. This approach can be used to explore academic problems and behavioral ones. Relative influence questions often begin with the exploration of the impact of the problem or difficulty on the student's learning or, more globally, on his or her life.

The dominant descriptions that young people use may not be the descriptions that they favor; they may very well prefer to create some other descriptions of themselves. Even if this may be desirable, it may not necessarily be within the realm of possibility for people who have lived according to the problem story for a significant part of their lives. Often, these stories completely eclipse any other description of ourselves that we would like to have.

During the next week, Jeremy broke his contract a number of times. Despite ongoing difficulties, however, he was looking forward to meeting Donna. In her next meeting with Jeremy, Donna asked, "Jeremy, when did this badness that you spoke of last week start to visit you?"

He thought for a minute, a little perplexed by the strange wording, and said in a hesitant and diffident tone, "I think it must have happened when I stole some money from my mother's purse."

Donna asked Jeremy about the effects of badness and how it made him feel. She asked for other examples of what badness made him do, all the time speaking in language that implied that "badness" was not necessarily a part of him as much as it was a "thing" outside of him that was making him do things he did not really want to do.

However much this goes against the grain of promoting self-responsibility, it does move discussion away from placing blame—a tendency that sabotages successful resolution of conflicts more than any other (J. Kottler, 1994).

Jeremy disclosed a full story of the effects of badness on his life and what it had done to him over time. He talked poignantly about all the things he missed because this badness kept him off guard. Jeremy became somewhat distressed and then a little outraged when he recognized what badness had talked him into about himself.

As a result of his conversations with Donna, he wanted to challenge badness by not listening to its efforts to tell him that he was sinful. Through careful questioning, Donna helped Jeremy recognize that badness had tricked him into believing that he was responsible for his parents' deaths and, recently, his grandfather's death. He shed numerous tears that related to both the devastation of losing his parents and grandfather and the burden that he had carried in feeling that he was to blame for their deaths.

Donna further elicited from Jeremy a number of skills and abilities he had used over the years to not let badness completely take over. He described the happy times he had with his grandfather in doing jobs for him. He spoke with warmth and pleasure about the times he helped plant the *kumara* (sweet potato) at a special time in the month when the moon was in the correct quarter.

Donna recognized that there was still considerable distress that Jeremy felt about his losses and that he was upset that he had not been able to attend the *tangi*. With Jeremy's permission, Donna arranged for him to meet with a *kaumatua* (Maori elder) who was a relative of Jeremy's. He was then taken to the cemetery where he could speak to his grandfather in the presence of the kaumatua, making this safe enough for him to feel many of his feelings and mixed emotions.

Meanwhile, Jeremy's behavior continued to be fairly erratic at school. He was absent from school for 2 or 3 days each week. Although some of the edge came off his intense activity in the classroom, he continued to be challenging to staff, and to Diana in particular.

Donna wanted to continue to support Jeremy and was able to arrange a way that she could meet with him a few more times. She asked Jeremy the following relative influence questions that explored the impact of dumbness on his life:

When did dumbness start to take effect at school? Was it soon after your meeting where you were tested, or did it slowly creep up on you?

How much would you say that dumbness has taken you over and how much do you have left of yourself that it has not taken yet? Has it got in the way of being with people that you want to be with?

Because Donna was developing a positive working relationship with Jeremy, she was able to find out a great deal about the effects of the dumbness story on him. Jeremy was surprised about how much dumbness had messed up many of his early ambitions; he decided for himself that he wanted things to be different. Although Donna wanted this outcome for Jeremy as well, it was important that Jeremy wanted this for himself because he would very likely slip into being a passenger in his life with others advocating for him on his own behalf.

Despite Jeremy's desire to let go of dumbness, his attendance at school remained intermittent for several months until he had a scare with the police resulting from petty thievery. He began to attend school more regularly but participated in only a few classes. With some genuine and enthusiastic persistence from Donna, Jeremy did have some plans for himself in which dumbness was not completely in charge.

Although there are limits to how much time, energy, and training that teachers have to pursue inquiries in such depth as this, this case does illustrate how, through patient listening and leading questions, it is possible to understand disruptive behavior in a completely different cultural context. If a trained narrative counselor was to take this case one step further—to go beyond mere understanding of Jeremy and his situation and attempt to intervene in such a way as to change his behavior—the process would continue to unfold as described in the following paragraphs.

Once the influence of the problem-related issue has been explored, the teacher or counselor would look for exceptions in which the person has not been totally controlled.

Donna asked Jeremy, "Have there been any times recently where you ignored dumbness briefly and learned something anyway?"

Jeremy replied after some time, "I can't think of anything." Finally, he said in a nonchalant voice, "I think I might go to college some day."

Donna saw this as a point of leverage. She quickly followed up: "How come dumbness was letting you even think about the possibilities of having a future for yourself?"

Other questions came flooding into Donna's mind: What was it about Jeremy's growing up that let him push dumbness out? Why was dumbness letting him think about learning? Everything had "sucked" in the past. Donna asked, "Are you sure that dumbness has destroyed any chance for you to appreciate any aspect of school life?"

Obviously, there was something that kept bringing Jeremy back to school. Donna felt that Jeremy was offering a tentative connection. Jeremy said in a hesitant and indecisive way, "Well, two subjects are okay." He was not convinced that he was learning much, but at least the classes were not boring. Cooking new things and finding out about things relating to food was pretty good. Donna was filled with further questions she was ready to ask. Did he read the recipes, measure the ingredients, follow instructions, and get a good result? Where was dumbness while this was happening?

Dumbness had been training Jeremy to believe he was a failure. It had not completely eclipsed his life, however. Jeremy agreed that there had been a few areas where it (dumbness) had not taken over.

Assembling the Alternative Story

Using a narrative approach, the teacher's task is to work with the student to assemble fragments of experience that the student believes are an example of what he or she would like to have more of in his or her life. Using these fragments, or favored moments, which have never been reflected on or noticed in the person's life, both teacher and student, as coauthors, carefully reconstruct them into an alternative and more enriching description of the student's story. This requires considerable skill and practice, but the results can be startling.

Donna asked, "Do you want dumbness to be more in charge, or do you want to be more in charge?" Jeremy said, "I don't want dumbness to be so strong," joining Donna with the use of the externalized metaphor. From their talks, Donna has assisted Jeremy to see how there were a number of areas of his life in which dumbness did not control him.

A month ago, Jeremy had successfully passed a difficult Maori language test after his second attempt. Donna helped Jeremy see how his own competencies had not let dumbness take him completely over. Rather than focus on the first failed test, which Jeremy initially slipped into doing, Donna asked him about how dumbness had not talked him out of taking the test again. Where had Jeremy developed the abilities to keep on trying in the face of defeat? How was he able to keep going to school despite the fact that so much of it had been punishing? Did he prefer the description of himself that dumbness painted, or was he more attracted to the picture that *he* was beginning to paint that featured Jeremy in the foreground and dumbness in the background? Who out of the people he knows would be least surprised about hearing this new description of himself? What did these changes in the way he saw himself mean for his future? The more Jeremy was given the opportunity to evaluate the direction that his life was taking, the more he began to take ownership of his future.

Teachers using the story metaphor develop a range of approaches to allowing the alternative, preferred story to come alive. For example, Donna was able to produce further questions that highlighted the emergence of this new description of Jeremy that he was beginning to incorporate into his life. When Jeremy considered who would be least surprised, he remembered that his grandfather had always loved him and felt that he was a special person who would do special things in his life. Given the opportunity to reflect on his positive relationship with his grandfather, he found himself wanting more for himself. He recognized that his future with dumbness being in charge was rather bleak. Jeremy, however, could gain a glimpse of the implications of his preferred story for the future.

Narrative Teaching and Cultural Sensitivity

There are several aspects about the story described in this chapter that are somewhat unique to its particular setting and context. After all, we are not in New Zealand, we do not have Maori students, nor do we have the training and luxury to chat with students to the extent that Donna was able to with Jeremy. Furthermore, one of the facets of this case that made Jeremy responsive to Donna, but not to his regular teacher, was that they were both members of the same culture.

Maybe what techniques Donna used mattered less than the fact that she was able to convince a student that she was on his side and that she understood his world because she was part of the same "tribe." One of the most difficult challenges for any teacher is to make contact with a student who is a member of a different cultural group, especially one that has a history of domination.

Embedded in narrative techniques, such as externalization and relative influence questions, is a state of mind in which the teacher attempts to understand the cultural worlds of children and to consider what they know and how they know it. Narrative teaching means being sensitive to how stories are constructed and, mostly, how they may be "coauthored" to form an altogether different perception of school, class activities, and student performance.

Jeremy may have been helped because narrative techniques are so powerful. Then again, it may have been the trusting relationship that Donna developed with him that made all the difference. Maybe it was both these strategies. Perhaps Jeremy changed because, for the first time in his life, he felt like he belonged in school. Regardless of how we do it, or with which methods we employ, our primary job as teachers is to help each child feel that he or she belongs in school and is capable of succeeding.

Note

1. The Maori *tangi* is a large communal funeral in which the person who has died lies in an open casket on the *Marae* (a sacred meeting place) and is surrounded by the *whanau* (extended family) for a period of 3 days. At Jeremy's grandfather's *tangi*, there were approximately 300 people in attendance. Typical of a *tangi*, many of the women elders set in motion a wailing cry that encourages the family to express their grief. The speeches given by the extended family and friends address the deceased in direct speech, expressing their honest views about him or her, including views on both the virtues and the faults of the person. Children are usually involved in all aspects of this ceremony.

Internationalizing
the Classroom

Elaine Jarchow
and
Jeffrey A. Kottler

One way that teachers can help students to personalize learning in culturally relevant ways is to create an international atmosphere in their classrooms. In this chapter, some creative methods for making cultural sensitivity more an integral part of daily activities at school are investigated.

Why Internationalize the Classroom?

The day is beginning at Future School, and Ms. Bishop, born in Ghana, and Mr. Hernandez, born in Bolivia, are team teaching in an exciting "international" classroom. The students themselves represent a variety of ethnic backgrounds and countries of origin. They approach all thematic units with a global perspective, whether they are working on math problems, health issues, or reading lessons. For example, in a class discussion on politics they examined Hong Kong in particular. Today, they will use the desktop video conferencing unit to talk to several individuals in Hong Kong about the impact they have felt since the transfer of power from Great Britain to China. Later, they will use electronic mail and bulletin boards to connect with teenagers around the world to discuss family customs. Part of the family unit has included reading books from many countries. The Internet has been a valuable resource to pursue research papers on global issues such as the environment.

The students agree that their internationalized classroom has helped them to understand themselves, each other, and their teachers from a perspective much larger than they ever could have imagined. The children now think in terms of how events affect not only them, their families, and their community but also the world at large. They understand their own cultures as part of a larger picture. They appreciate the unique features of each ethnic, religious, and cultural group represented in their school, but they also see a number of commonalities that unite all people in universal goals. They see themselves as citizens of the world, committed to make an impact on a global scale, whether through commerce, communication, or travel.

Considering that only approximately 5% of kindergarten through 12th-grade teachers have any academic preparation in global studies, it is no wonder that our schools are not preparing young people to participate effectively in a more culturally diverse and increasingly dependent world (Merryfield & Harris, 1992). When a more international approach to education is taken, however, students are helped to understand the rich diversity and complexity of the world and how interdependent we are on one another. They learn to be more collaborative in their thinking and behavior (Merryfield, 1996a, 1996b).

A number of other benefits may result from internationalizing the classroom, including the following:

1. It promotes equity and social justice, especially using knowledge and skills for decision making and social and political action against structural inequalities and oppression (Alexandre,

1988; Cushner, McClelland, & Safford, 1992; DeKock, 1989; Drum & Howard, 1989; Kobus & Rojas, 1988; Wilson, 1996).

2. It improves intergroup relations, promoting intercultural competence, and building community across cultures (Bennett & Bennett, 1994; Cortés, 1979; Fain, 1988; Wilson, 1996).

3. It reduces stereotyping, prejudice, and discrimination (Bennett, 1995; Cortés, 1979).

4. It promotes a knowledge of human diversity and human commonalities (Cortés, 1979; Cushner et al., 1992; Wilson, 1996).

5. It stimulates a knowledge for cultural consciousness of one's own and other cultures (Bennett, 1995; Bennett & Bennett, 1994; Wilson, 1996).

6. It allows access to knowledge from multiple perspectives (particularly perspectives of people on the margins economically, politically, or culturally) and skills in critical understanding of the process of knowledge construction (Banks, 1995; Kobus, 1989/1990; Said, 1993; Wilson, 1993).

Clearly, there are a number of reasons to consider making your instruction more international in perspective. The best reason of all, however, is that it makes learning more fun.

When Teachers Model
an International Perspective

Our interest in global education has formed over 30 years of travel, work, and study in many countries. As teacher educators, we are more and more convinced that the future of our field is based on expanding our views of education in such a way that we consider the policies and practices employed all over the globe. We have been advocates for student exchanges, faculty exchanges, and field placements abroad. When colleagues and school district officials argued that it made little sense to send student teachers abroad when they desperately needed experience on a local level, we fought hard to make international opportunities available anyway. We knew from personal experience the kinds of transformative changes that are possible only when living and working in another culture. We knew exactly the kind of flexibility and confidence that such experiences would develop in beginning teachers.

The enthusiasm that we feel for the possibilities inherent in global education is based not only on reviews of literature but also on personal experiences that have changed our lives. Before we examine some of the specifics of what teachers can do in their classrooms to make them more international in perspective, we share a sampling of critical incidents that we have experienced while working abroad.

Speech Night in New Zealand
(Elaine Jarchow)

Every year in October, the primary students at Hukanui Primary School in Hamilton, New Zealand, gear up for a collaborative competition known as Speech Night. The students write 3-minute speeches and present them to their classmates. Ultimately, student representatives from each class in the same grade level compete against each other in an evening session to which parents and siblings are invited. During my semester exchange in New Zealand, my then 9-year-old daughter competed in her third form class. What impressed me was the way in which the teacher "internationalized" the event. Sure, it was a competition, but during the evening finals all the students turned out to support the finalists. When my daughter stood up to speak, she dropped all her index cards. Immediately, several other contestants jumped up, retrieved and sorted the cards, and handed them to her. Somehow, the teacher had developed a collaborative atmosphere in which all the students felt committed to take care of one another. From that night onward, I vowed to incorporate a more global approach to any teaching I would do.

The School Without Walls
(Jeffrey A. Kottler)

While I had been doing consulting work in the Philippines, I had been asked to give a talk to a group of students at a small college in Manila. I showed up eager to pass along whatever wisdom that I could about my assigned topic, the human dimensions of teaching, within the brief time I had been allocated.

I was surprised to see that the building we were meeting in had an open-air feeling about it, even though we were smack in the middle of the most congested city on earth. As I stood on stage to address my audience, I was overwhelmed with the strange sights within my view. I could not help but notice that there was no back wall to the room, so I could see hundreds of spectators walking by, occasionally peaking inside. Cars, trucks, bicycles, jeepneys, and motorcycles continued to roar by, honking their horns. The noise and chaos made it difficult for me to think clearly. It was like I was standing on the busiest street corner, in the most congested part of any city, giving a speech.

Then, before I could begin my talk, a young student came on stage and sang a song—a ritual that was to be repeated four other times during the afternoon, always cued by something I could never quite identify. Somehow, I was able to ignore the distractions around me and launched into my talk until, inexplicably, the students filed out and another group walked in and sat down. Of course, this called for another song.

I was told that now I was speaking to nursing students instead of prospective teachers so I had to make some adjustments in my talk—that is, until another group changed places with the nurses. Throughout that afternoon, I continued to talk about human dimensions of teaching, nursing, social work, and a few other variations, each segment spiced up with a song. Throughout this experience, I was struck by how different the educational setting and rituals were compared to what I was used to. When I finally walked off that stage, to the accompaniment of another song, I wondered what the students learned from that encounter, and I took many months to digest what I had learned as well.

"Good Morning and Welcome" in Japan
(Elaine Jarchow)

No wonder Japanese children look forward to school! During my extended visit to Japan as part of a group research project to study their educational methods, I lived with a family consisting of a father, mother, teenager, and first grader.

During my stay with this family, I joined them in their usual activities and rituals. Among all the things that I saw and did there, what most stands out for me was the time I accompanied the first grader and his parents to the bus stop. This seemed to be a very grave and important moment in their lives, so I was most grateful for the privilege to share it with them.

We waited in the presence of a few other children, each of them escorted by both their parents. The bus arrived and who should step out to greet them but the teacher! She bowed to the parents, then to each child, and lovingly welcomed them aboard the bus.

School in Paradise
(Jeffrey A. Kottler)

Northern Queensland is a remote part of Australia where many of the Aboriginal reserves are located. I was working at one of the reserve schools for a few days that was located on a spectacular beach right off the Great Barrier Reef. Apparently, many years ago when the Aboriginals were herded off their land to be resettled out of view, the settlers neglected to check what lay over the mountain.

The setting for this school was simply spectacular. I saw children doing their assignments while lying under picnic tables on the beach. When I asked them why they were not in the water, they explained that there was a 20-foot saltwater crocodile that was currently patrolling the waters (now *that* is an excellent discipline method, I mused).

Later during my tour, I noticed an ominous-looking sign prominently displayed on a bulletin board: WARNING: A DEATH ADDER HAS BEEN SPOTTED IN THE CEMETERY. PLEASE STAY AWAY. A death adder, I had previously learned, was one of the most poisonous snakes in the world. One little lick and you are history.

The teacher who was with me at the time started chuckling as she saw me reading the sign. She said, "You know kids, as soon as they saw that, they immediately went to find the snake." Yes, I thought, I do know kids, and whether they are in the outback of Australia, or anywhere else, they cannot resist being curious.

A Great Day in India
(Elaine Jarchow)

Neshta is a small agricultural village of 200 families located on the India-Pakistan border. Several colleagues and I spent a day with the primary school children, their teachers, and their families. School was an extension of the village. Children worked together with their families to create gifts for the visitors and lovingly showed off their homes, temples, and work enterprises. They offered food, drink, and a rare look into their everyday life. As we boarded the bus to go home, the primary-school principal said, "These people will remember this day for the rest of their lives."

Making Learning Last

What school experiences are worth remembering for the rest of a student's life? So often, they involve some interaction with a foreign culture, one that challenges our assumptions and tests our most cherished beliefs. Teachers at all levels can internationalize their classrooms, and it is not necessary to be a frequent flyer to do so.

International encounters, whether they involve travel abroad, hosting visitors, or interacting through media, help to shape our worldviews and to make us more open, trusting, tolerant, caring, and more willing to look at things from multiple perspectives. As teachers, we must have cross-cultural experiences in both North America and other continents. This base of experience helps us to shape our international classroom.

The classroom itself should be a place in which curiosity and tolerance predominate. All units should include a global perspective, one in which alternative frames of reference are illustrated and alternative views of reality are demonstrated. Often, it is not necessary to travel very far to recruit resources in this area because the local community is a rich resource for international speakers—those from other countries or who have visited faraway lands.

These speakers can help students to understand not only global issues but also different customs. For example, Arab and Israeli students from a nearby university might shed some light on the current Arab-Israeli peace talks. A visitor from Ghana could help elementary school children know more about the songs, games, and dress of this West African nation. International electronic mail pen pals can help students ask questions and discuss current issues.

The framework for the international classroom is basically a simple one. The teacher with an enhanced worldview, shaped by cross-cultural experiences, internationalizes the classroom by providing thematic units and curriculum activities that encourage students to develop global perspectives. To stimulate your imaginations, we will briefly describe several different kinds of activities that can be used in elementary or secondary settings. These methods and resources (identified by Sally Pickert of Catholic University) are intended to help you develop others that fit more specifically to your particular needs.

Activities for the
Elementary School Classroom

1. The Metropolitan Museum of Art publishes a "Fun With Hieroglyphs" package that includes stamps that represent the hieroglyphic alphabet and suggested lessons. A first lesson shows children how to stamp secret messages. They learn to say "Happy Birthday," or "Thank You."

Later, students learn to read Egyptian names and associate them with their English equivalents. Students are also encouraged to do hieroglyphic crossword puzzles (Roehrig, 1990).

2. Several teachers at the Joshua Eaton Elementary School in Reading, Massachusetts, began their globalizing efforts by attending a China seminar at the Peabody Museum in Salem, Massachusetts. They then designed an interdisciplinary unit on maritime studies for fifth-grade students. Students learned about the Hawaiian, Japanese, and Chinese cultures that New England sailors encountered in the 19th century. Field trips to the Peabody Museum assisted the students as an impetus for their own explorations (Tye, 1990).

3. Among the best sources for ideas to internationalize the classroom is a book by Kirchner (1991) that describes several active games that keep children moving around. Each of these activities originates in a different country and teaches children about how others around the world play.

In Botswana, for example, they play a game called Hidden Object, in which one child hides his or her eyes while the others hide a small object such as a nut or coin. The child is then instructed to open his or her eyes while the other children begin singing a favorite song. As the searcher begins looking for the object, the others sing louder or softer depending on whether he or she is getting closer to or farther away from the object. Once the object is discovered, another child becomes the searcher and another song is chosen.

4. The East Asia Resource Center at the University of Washington publishes *Modern Japan: An Idea Book for K-12 Teachers* (Bernson & Magnusson, 1989). The Japanese culture offers many wonderful ideas for global education activities. The following are several that appeal to elementary school children.

Daruma Toys and Games

Gail Tokunaga

Materials needed: oval balloons, newspaper, wheat paste, paint, and brushes.

Procedures:

1. Explain to students that the daruma is Japan's best-known folk toy. You can see it anywhere in Japan, including on key rings. Daruma is short for Bodhidharma, a Buddhist priest from India who lived in the sixth century. Legends say that Bodhidharma sat absolutely still and meditated for 9 years. He did not move at all, and after 9 years he found that he had lost the use of his arms and legs. In fact, they had withered away.

   Therefore, darumas are made with no arms or legs. They have weighted bottoms so that no matter how you roll them, they will always return right side up. Some say this symbolizes the spirit of patience, perseverance, and determination shown by the priest.

   There are many kinds of darumas, and they are painted different ways in different parts of Japan. Traditionally, they are made without eyes. When you make a wish, you paint on one eye. When the wish comes true, you paint in the other eye.
2. Blow up an oval balloon.
3. Tear up many strips of paper and soak them in wheat paste. Cover the balloon completely with the strips. Let dry.
4. Add extra layers of strips to the bottom, rounded end. This will give the bottom the extra weight it needs so that the daruma will end up in an upright position.

5. The daruma is traditionally painted red, the color of the robes worn by the priests. Paint the body and the features on the face. Remember not to paint the eyes yet.
6. Make a wish and paint one eye. Be patient.
7. When the wish comes true, paint the other eye.

Activities for the
Junior or Senior High School

1. The *Arab World Notebook* (Shabbas & Al-Qazzaz, 1989) is a rich resource of activities that help students understand Middle Eastern culture. The following are a few of those that are described.

Equivalent Proverbs

Proverbs share a number of characteristics. They are current: people, in general, use and understand them. They are pithy: short and snappy thoughts expressed in a minimum of words. They often, although not always, contain elements such as rhyme, rhythm, and figures of speech. A proverb may take the form of a declarative sentence, an exhortation, an invocation, a curse, an oath, or a riddle followed by its answer.

A proverb is a special kind of speech that differs from everyday conversation. An Arab can tell you when something is or is not a proverb but, like most of us when it comes to proverbs, has trouble explaining just how he or she knows. The richest source of Arabic proverbs is the *Quran*. Arabic proverbs tell us a great deal about life in the region—the domestic cycle, kinship, marriage, child rearing, and marriage patterns characteristic of this part of the world.

The following are examples of Arab proverbs:

Children are the wealth of the Arabs.
A house without a child is like a house without a light.
Avoid greed, and poverty will avoid you.
Mind your own business and you'll see no evil.
Once your son grows up, treat him as a brother.
The best among you are those who are best to their womenfolk.
Feed the hungry, visit the sick, and free the captive.

Often, an Arabic proverb will appear to have an equivalent in English. Sometimes, it is almost an exact equivalent, as in the following Arabic proverbs:

If speech is silver, then silence is golden.
He whose house is made of glass should not throw stones.

Other Arabic proverbs have near-equivalents, which you can determine for yourselves. Can you state the English near-equivalent of the following Arabic proverbs? [Teacher: The following are some Arabic proverbs and some near-equivalents to serve as an answer key. Your students will come up with even more. Cover the right side and duplicate the proverbs so that only the Arabic ones appear. This exercise will lead naturally into similarities of cultural values]

Arabic Proverb	*English Near-Equivalent*
What comes with ease goes with ease.	Easy come easy go.
Man plans and God manages.	Man proposes but God disposes.
Too many cooks burn the food.	Too many cooks spoil the broth.
Love is blind.	Love is blind.
Time is gold.	Time is money.
Don't cut the tree that shades you.	Don't bite the hand that feeds you.

2. Some of Kirchner's (1991) games can also be adapted for older kids in the regular or physical education classroom. In Foot Searching, from Belgium, five children lie on their backs, one behind the other, in a straight line. The children try to pass a beanbag, using only their feet, backward to the next person. If someone drops the beanbag, it is returned to the front and the game continues. As soon as the beanbag arrives at the last child, he or she runs to the front of the line, lies down, and starts the process again. The game is over when the first child arrives again at the beginning of the row.

3. In One-Legged Concentration, from South Africa, one ball or beanbag and four traffic cones are used. The four traffic cones are arranged in a square and one player is placed in the middle. Each of the other four players are stationed next to one of the traffic cones.

The player in the center has a beanbag or ball and calls out, "Go!" Every player, including the center player, starts hopping on one leg to a different traffic cone. The player with the beanbag can throw it to another player at any time. Players cannot stop hopping until they reach another traffic cone, so they have to catch the beanbag while moving.

If a fair throw is made and a player catches it, he or she gets one point. If the player drops or misses the beanbag, he or she loses one point and must pick it up and throw it to another player. Two or more players cannot be at a cone at the same time. The game is restarted when all players are at a cone. The player who receives 10 points first wins the game.

4. To encourage comparison of cultures, Pikering (1990) allows students to compare and contrast three to five diverse cultures; to identify factors influencing cultural development; to create a new culture; and to learn to work cooperatively. In the unit on Bolivia, students are asked to think about cultural similarities and differences with respect to food, clothing, housing, language, religion, government, transportation, and education. The following are some excerpts from a letter that a young Bolivian girl has written to her sister. Imagine a group of your secondary students reading the letter and discussing cultural similarities and differences.

La Paz, Bolivia
January 15

Dear Paulina,

I miss you very much. I wish I were old enough to come to Tambillo to work on the farm with you. Are you weeding the potatoes and carrots, or does Uncle Alberto have you tending the llamas and sheep?

This morning before father caught the bus for Villa Tajedae, where he is working on a house, he talked to me again about how important going to school is. . . . I want to do well in school. I worry that father and mother won't have enough money to send me to intermediate school. I'm sorry they weren't able to send you to high school; I know you were looking forward to being a teacher.

Since you moved to Tambillo, I have had to do more work at home. I don't mind getting the water every morning at the community tap, because I can visit with Maria. I do hate whitewashing our adobe walls, though.

I've been playing a game with Edgar and part of the game includes having him sweep the dirt floor.

I went to the public health clinic the other day to get my diphtheria shot. The doctor was nice, and asked me all kinds of questions about everyone in our family. He asked about what we ate, then told me we should try to eat more protein. I know he is right, but it is hard when meat and fish are so expensive. I think that is why mother feels so weak all the time.

Father says our country is much better off than when the military was in control. He is afraid there will be another attempt to get rid of the president, though, because there are so many problems. Too many people are trying to come to live in La Paz. Father says that is one of the reasons he is having such a hard time getting work as a carpenter.

Mother has been saving up money for over a month so we can have *empanada saltena*. She is allowing me to fix it for the first time. I remember that it was one of your favorite meals.

I must stop writing and send this to you.

Love,
Constancia

With this letter, or any similar stimulus, students are helped to move beyond their own worlds and experiences to enter cultures different from their own. This not only helps students adopt a more global approach to solving life's problems but also encourages them to be more inquisitive and tolerant of one another's cultural differences.

Our intent in presenting these few examples of activities to promote a more international classroom is to show how almost any unit, lesson, or subject can be infused with greater appreciation for cultural differences. As mentioned in previous chapters, it is not so much the specific techniques that matter as much as the atmosphere that is created, especially one in which children are encouraged to look at everything with an inquisitive mind that asks, "I wonder how they would do that in other parts of the world."

Additional Resources

American Forum for Global Education (120 Wall Street, Suite 2600, New York, NY 10005. Phone: (212) 742-8232; Fax: (212) 742-8752). This is a nonprofit organization acting as a resource center on global education, and it administers the National Clearinghouse on Development Education. The Forum is part of the International Network for Global Education, which promotes teaching about global issues worldwide.

Anderson, C., Nicklas, S., & Crawford, A. (1994). *Global understandings: A framework for teaching and learning.* Alexandria, VA: Association for Supervision and Curriculum Development. This book provides a framework for global education along with sample integrated units, performance assessment suggestions, and an appendix of resources including toys and curriculum materials for children.

Choices for the 21st Century (Watson Institute for International Studies, Brown University, Box 1948, Providence, RI 02912-1948. Phone: (401) 863-3155; Fax: (401) 863-1247; Internet address: choices@brown.edu). This group publishes curriculum units for Grades 9 through 12 on current international relations issues developed by the Choices for the 21st Century Education Project at the Watson Institute for International Studies, Brown University.

Culturgrams (David M. Kennedy Center for International Studies–Publication Services, Brigham Young University, 280 Harold R. Clark Bldg., Provo, UT 84602-4538. Phone: (800) 528-6279 or (801) 378-6528; Fax: (801) 378-7075; Internet address: David Deem@byu.edu). Culturgrams are four-page briefings that discuss a nation's background and society, as well as the customs, courtesies, and lifestyles of its people. These are ideal for educators, students, community leaders, and anyone interested in the daily lives of the people in a given nation. Available individually or in sets. Call (800) 528-6279 for a free sample and catalog.

Global Learning, Inc. (1018 Stuyvesant Avenue, Union, NJ 07083. Phone: (908) 964-1114; Fax: (908) 964-6335). This company produces curriculum materials for kindergarten through college and conducts teacher education workshops for exploring issues of global interdependence such as sustainable development and conflict resolution and mediation.

Global Pages (Immaculate Heart College, 425 Shatto Place, Suite 401, Los Angeles, CA 90020. Phone: (213) 386-3116; Fax: (213) 386-6334). This is a quarterly publication of special reports, curriculum materials, and classroom exercises about peace, justice, and global cooperation. It is designed for Grade 9 and higher.

Hartoonian, H. M., & Stock, H. (1992). *A guide to curriculum planning in global studies*. Madison: Wisconsin State Department of Public Instruction. This guide is designed to assist educators develop curricula to embrace global perspectives, including an overview of global studies, themes and topics of global studies, and sample teaching units.

International Classroom (University of Pennsylvania, 33rd and Spruce Streets, University Museum of Archaeology and Anthropology, Philadelphia, PA, 19104. Phone: (215) 898-4066). As an educational resource organization, International Classroom promotes a multicultural educational program for people of all cultures to share stories of their countries and culture.

Social Science Education Consortium, Inc. (SSEC) (P.O. Box 21270, Boulder, CO 80308-4270. Phone: (303) 492-8154). SSEC publishes books for teaching social sciences in kindergarten through 12th-grade classrooms including resource, curriculum, and teaching guides on global issues and world history.

Social Studies Development Center (SSDC) (Indiana University, 2805 E. 10th Street, Bloomington, IN 47408. Phone: (812) 335-3838). SSDC promotes research focused on social studies and global studies education and provides instructional materials on global issues.

Social Studies School Service (10200 Jefferson Boulevard, P.O. Box 802, Culver City, CA 90232-0802. Phone: (310) 839-2436; Fax: (310) 829-2249). This group distributes curriculum materials on topics such as the environment, global economics, international relations, and geography.

Stanford Program on International and Cross-Cultural Education (SPICE) (Stanford University, 300 Littlefield Center, Room 14, 300 Lausen Street, Stanford, CA 94305. Phone: (415) 723-1114; Fax: (415) 723-6784). SPICE provides curriculum materials for teaching various global units.

Tye, K. (Ed.). (1990). *Global education: School-based strategies.* Orange, CA: Interdependence Press. The book provides examples of how schools have introduced global education to their students.

10

What Matters Most

Throughout *What's Really Said in the Teachers' Lounge,* I have presented some provocative ideas designed to stimulate reflection and discussion related to the subject of culture and the classroom. Although national conferences have cultural themes, journals are loaded with culturally sensitive literature, curricula mandate training for culturally diverse populations, and school districts require in-service programs on multicultural subjects, we are still not doing nearly enough. We talk in the language of the multiculturally fluent without really confronting our own cultures and how they affect our work with others.

What is it that really matters most in our work with children? When we speak of educating young people, what is it that we most want them to learn? In Chapter 9, an anecdote was shared about the effort that is made in Japan to make children feel welcome in their schools. What about our children, especially those who are members of minority cultures? To what extent do they feel that our classrooms belong to them?

Not Feeling Welcome

In the Cairns region of Northeast Australia, home to many
Aboriginals and Torres Strait Islanders (from the islands between
Papua New Guinea and Australia), the government has recruited the
assistance of a dozen indigenous workers who roam the schools in
the vicinity. Their job is to serve as roving consultants on things
Aboriginal—to educate teachers about their culture, to mediate disputes between indigenous parents and school authorities, and to
serve as mentors for children who rarely make it to high school, let
alone graduate. They act as advocates for the minority students,
supporting them as much as possible.

Often, these educational consultants sit in on classrooms, making
themselves as unobtrusive as possible. During one such observation,
an indigenous consultant witnessed a teacher censuring an Aboriginal student for interrupting her before she was through talking.
During this rebuke, another student, a white student, interrupted the
teacher as she was completing her thoughts. She actually turned to
this student, smiled indulgently, answered his question, and then
resumed her lecture about the rudeness of interrupting. The consultant was so shocked by this obvious double standard, that she sat
speechless during the encounter. She wondered about not only the
obvious biases of the teacher but also the assumptions students hold
about what is appropriate. Here, the teacher is scolding a black child
about interruptions and it never occurs to the white student that such
rules would apply to him as well.

Although this is an extreme example of teacher prejudice, the
Aboriginal consultant says she sees this kind of thing all the time.
Minority kids do not stay in school in Australia, North America, or
anywhere in the world because they see the place as alien territory.

As enlightened as we might see ourselves and as culturally
sensitive as we might claim to be, each of us is continuously making
certain students not feel welcome in our classrooms. We do this by
subtle means. We do this under the guise of setting standards or
enforcing boundaries. Most of all, we do this because each of us holds
biases in favor of some students and against others. Whereas some
students earn our wrath or respect, others inherit our feelings based
on attitudes we hold toward their particular gender and culture. We
can deny this all we like—claim to be exempt from such prejudices,
point fingers elsewhere, make excuses, and disown responsibility—

but the fact remains that every teacher on this planet has strong preferences toward those students whom he or she would prefer to teach. Some of these preferences are based on individual characteristics; others are based on skin color, physical attributes, and cultural patterns.

Some students do not feel welcome in our classrooms because they sense our disapproval toward their particular cultural behaviors. Others misread us, assume that we do not like them, when they are actually judging us with the same prejudicial attitudes that they accuse us of holding. In either case, continuous miscommunications and misunderstandings are likely.

Those Who Are Misunderstood

According to some estimates, one in every four American Indian children born on certain reservations suffers the effects of fetal alcohol syndrome (FAS). This means that a significant segment of the school population in these areas is showing some degree of mental impairment, problems of impulse control, and neurological disorders that are directly related to maternal alcohol use during pregnancy. Because these effects can manifest themselves at varying levels of impairment, many behaviors among Indian children that may appear to be hostile, resistant, unmotivated, or delinquent may, in fact, be the result of physiological disorders associated with prenatal alcohol consumption.

Speaking about his own adopted son, who is the victim of FAS, Dorris (1989) writes,

My son will forever travel through a moonless night with only the roar of the wind for company. Don't talk to him of mountains, of tropical beaches. Don't ask him to swoon at sunrises or marvel at the filter of light through leaves. He's never had time for such things, and he does not believe in them. He may pass by them close enough to touch them on either side, but his hands are stretched forward, grasping for balance instead of pleasure. He doesn't wonder where he came from, where he's going. He doesn't ask who he is, or why. Questions are a luxury, the province of those at a distance from the periodic shock of rain. Gravity presses

Adam so hard against reality that he doesn't feel the point at which he touches it. A drowning man is not separated from the lust for air by a bridge of thought—he is one with it—and my son, conceived and grown in an ethanol bath, lives each day in the act of drowning. For him there is no shore. (p. 264)

Throughout Adam's whole educational career, he was misunderstood by his teachers. Rarely did anyone consider that his erratic behavior and poor school performance might be due to something other than being a lazy, unmotivated Indian. There is, after all, a history of educators neglecting to consider biological influences on behavior, just as there has been a failure to look at cultural factors.

In a review of how teachers all but ignore research on physiological processes involved in learning, Hancock (1996) mentions just a few archaic methods, beginning with the whole school schedule. For example, once children hit puberty, their sleep cycle changes in a way that optimal learning takes place in the late morning. In one study that compared teens beginning school at 7:30 a.m. or at 9:30 a.m., the ones who started earlier did worse in school.

Another example is related to language acquisition. Typically, foreign languages are taught to children beginning in 9th or 10th grade, a period when, biologically speaking, the optimal window for learning without an accent has already been closed. Still other examples relate to how music and physical exercise are critical to learning processes at every stage of development.

In addition to being wedded to obsolete traditions in our schools by ignoring brain research, we also neglect cultural learning styles. Am I suggesting that we must make a hundred adaptions in how we teach according to each child's culture and preferences? Yes and no.

To the extent that flexibility is possible, a policy of maximum choices in how material is learned is certainly a good thing. Everyone enjoys the freedom to learn a task with methods that are ideally suited to his or her style. Overadapting to student needs, however, is neither practical for teachers who are already overwhelmed nor ultimately serving the students best.

Just because students of various cultures learn in different ways does not mean that they cannot add to their repertoire. In a world that values some learning styles over others and that requires people to be able to grasp new information quickly by reading, listening, or viewing a computer screen, we have a responsibility to teach children to do these things well. Multiple-choice testing, for example, may be culturally biased, but many sectors of the world offer opportunities based on successful performance on these measures. It is our job to teach children, especially those who are test handicapped, to learn the skills involved in decoding objective questions. Likewise, some children may have been enculturated not to challenge teachers, whereas others are encouraged to speak their minds. Both response styles are useful, depending on the context; both types of students need to learn the other's style if they are to succeed in our increasingly multicultural community.

It may very well be that what you do on the outside might not change as much as what you think and feel on the inside. It is still important to teach all children how to sit quietly and how to work cooperatively in groups. It is useful that all children should master the intricacies of learning through imagery, verbalization, analytic reasoning, class discussion, repetitive drills, artistic representation, physical movement, and so on.

You may very well hardly change the overall structures of how you design your curriculum and manage your classroom. You surely can interpret children's behavior in a whole new light, however. Kids who you previously believed were unmotivated, resistant, and uncooperative may very well be struggling with a structure that they are unable to fit into, even if they desperately want to.

When Teachers Have Trouble

Several years ago, I was feeling burned out by my work as a therapist and teacher. It seemed to me that every child sent to me to be fixed was a difficult, resistant case. In my darkest moments, I really did believe that these kids stayed up late at night plotting ways to make my life miserable. In fact, I was so disturbed by these disruptive, uncooperative people that I decided to write a book about them that I initially titled *Clients From Hell.* I believed that this would be greatly needed because we all deal with such individuals who are manipulative, hostile, withdrawn, or even sociopathic.

Each chapter was going to be about a different student from hell—the kid who plagues you with a series of irritating actions, each of which is intended to get underneath your skin; the one who challenges your authority by screaming "Fuck you!" in your face; the child who just sits in class doing nothing except breathing, and sometimes you even wonder about that; the one who has suffered from abuse to the point that trust is out of the question; and the child from a strange culture that sabotages any effort on your part to be helpful. I am sure you have your favorite list of nominations as well.

Obviously, this subject of dealing with difficult students has immediate appeal, worthy of its own book rather than simple honorable mention (Kottler, 1997a). I knew I was on to something important because we spend so much of our lives talking about these kids, complaining about what they are doing to us, utterly at a loss to explain why they are so uncooperative, mean-spirited, or unmotivated.

One of the reviewers of the first draft of *Clients From Hell* said something to me I will never forget. In very careful, diplomatic prose he said to me: "Kottler, I think you might have a problem. You speak of these people you are trying to help as if they were sent from hell to make your life miserable."

Yes! I heartily agreed. That is *exactly* what it feels like. These kids *are* the plague of my life.

It immediately reminded me of a story I wanted to tell this reviewer on the spot. "You wouldn't believe this child I saw today . . ."

The reviewer, however, continued with a question that froze my thinking in its tracks. He asked me, softly but directly: Where was my compassion for these people? Indeed, I had started thinking about the troubled children as enemies to be defeated rather than as people reaching out for help in the only way they knew how. I renamed the book *Compassionate Therapy.*

Students who we find most difficult, you see, are not doing anything to us (even though it often feels that way) but rather to themselves. Furthermore, they are not so much being resistant as they are trying to cooperate with us in a way that might most generously be reframed as "unusual." There are reasons for this, of course, and most of the reasons have to do with our not really understanding the children's cultural context for their behavior.

Therefore, why do we struggle so mightily with some children who are not being as cooperative as we prefer? The answer could be found in one of the following possibilities (Kottler, 1992, 1997a):

1. The students want to cooperate, but they cannot because of some underlying physical condition such as attention deficit disorder, hyperactivity, or a biologically based depression.
2. I mentioned in a previous chapter how you might be missing some information about the student that leads you to make assumptions that are not necessarily valid. For example, what may look to you like resistance may be an attempt on the part of a student to protect himself or herself.
3. You inadvertently provoked a student by a remark or action that was perceived as insensitive. For instance, you called on a student to give an answer to a question. Even though the student knew the answer, he or she would lose face in front of his or her peers by showing that he or she really is prepared (the student is part of a culture that devalues being smart in school). Instead, the student was forced to say that he or she did not know, losing face in another way.
4. Your own culture makes it difficult for you to be as flexible as you need to be to reach those students who hold very different beliefs and values. Imagine, for instance, that a student comes from a culture in which admitting that she knows something would be construed as arrogance and a lack of humility. This is in direct opposition to your own values in which a female, if she is going to get anywhere in this world, has got to be assertive.

To reach those students you experience as most difficult, you must be willing to examine not only their behavior and what it is doing to you but also your own culture.

So, What Matters Most?

Certainly compassion matters a lot in your work with students who come from cultures that are different from your own. Compassion and empathy are what permit you to build the kinds of relationships you will need if you are ever going to bridge the miscommunications and misunderstandings that are inevitable in such cultural clashes. When one culture (yours) is committed to goals of responsibility, productivity, and achievement, and the other culture (theirs) is committed to having fun and staying entertained, then disagreements are likely.

Your genuine interest in children's cultures communicates essential respect and kindness. There is nothing more inviting than an adult who communicates the following to a child:

> I don't know nearly enough about who you are and where you are but I want to know very much. Would you help educate me about your world? Will you help me to understand where you come from? Would you also be patient with me when I make mistakes? Would you please help me to become more sensitive to your needs and interests? Oh yes . . . one more thing . . . would you please do me the honor of treating me exactly the same way that I am treating you?

Although qualities such as compassion, caring, and essential kindness cannot be overrated, they are hardly enough. More than a few times, we have been walked all over, if not abused, because our caring was interpreted by some as weakness to be exploited. Certainly, setting negotiated rules and boundaries is critical when (a) they are enforced fairly and consistently, (b) they have been devised through negotiation with those who must live by them, and (c) they are responsive to the cultural differences of those in the room.

A certain degree of doubt and uncertainty also matters quite a bit. It is when we think we know things, when we are absolutely positive that things are a particular way, that we come across as arrogant and rigid. In fact, what we think we know and understand usually fits only within the epistemological base of our own internal cultures. I am certain, for example, that learning history is a good thing. It helps us learn from the past. It is part of what I consider to be a truly educated person. I have learned the hard way, however, more than a few times, that history gets in the way for some people who refuse to live in the present. Furthermore, what I consider to be accurate history bears little resemblance to what others might think.

I once went on a tour of Corregidor Island in the Philippines, the site where the most ferocious battles of the Pacific were fought. This is where General MacArthur made his stand against the Japanese and near where the Bataan Death March took place. It is where first the Filipinos and their American allies made a courageous stand, then the Japanese took over and tried to hold the island against the Allies, and then again the Americans invaded, only to be subjected to fierce invasions and bombardments. Corregidor is a name that has a significant place in both American and Japanese history.

During my tour, I was surprised to see that we were divided into two groups. The Japanese tourists were sent one way, to be given their own tour of the island with a Japanese interpreter and historian. They were told about the honor and courage their ancestors had shown in these battles. They were regaled by stories in which their soldiers outmaneuvered and outfoxed their American and Filipino counterparts, losing only because of inadequate resources. This was an interesting interpretation of history because on our tour group, which was composed of Americans and Filipinos, we were told about the cowardly and immoral actions on the part of the Japanese. At one point on the island, the two groups met at the same spot, a high cliff where hundreds of Japanese soldiers jumped to their deaths rather than surrender. The Japanese tourists were told about this incident as one of the honorable and bravest gestures on the part of their people. My group, however, heard from our guide about how senseless this waste of human life was—a complete act of desperation. All history is written in just this way—from different perspectives of each culture. It is doubt and uncertainty, therefore, that keep us humble.

Flexibility matters a lot. There are distinctly different learning styles evident in how children of various cultures process and remember new information. While reflecting on the trouble one of his Indian students was having learning basic concepts in civics class, More (1993) noted that, whereas in class details are ordinarily presented first, leading up to an overall scheme, at home this student was taught by her grandfather in terms of global images with details filled in later. More began thinking about a number of other characteristic styles by which children of certain cultures learn best. This, of course, has implications for the instruction of even homogeneous groups because it has been noted repeatedly how each child has particular strengths and weaknesses in grasping abstractions, verbal images, mechanical sequences, analytic reasoning, or perhaps cooperative learning assignments.

Generally speaking, an Asian student might compete in timed assignments more effectively than others, just as African Americans might excel in reality-based split-second decision making or an

American Indian might do better in group tasks. Although it is dangerous to make too many assumptions about learning styles on the basis of cultural factors alone, it is helpful to reflect on the reasons why certain children struggle with particular school tasks.

There have been fears raised by opponents of multicultural curricula in schools who see the movement as contributing to greater factionalism, hostility, and resentment by people of different races. Much depends, however, on what the intent of this movement is: "Is it to promote harmony and an acceptance of our society? Or to portray our society as so fatally flawed by racism, so irreparably unfair and unequal that it must be rejected as evil?" (Glazer, 1993, p. 19).

The same question could be asked, of course, about any ideology or educational method. In some hands, multiculturalism becomes a means to justify conflict, compensatory oppression, reverse racism, and intellectual dishonesty. When used judiciously, culturally relative and sensitive education is the only way we can respond legitimately to the changing nature of our population. This means not only exploring the worlds of our children but also acknowledging and understanding our own cultures and their influence on our behavior. Most of all, it means bringing our most private conversations out of the teachers' lounge, scrutinizing our most honest beliefs and provocative ideas, and facing ourselves and our students with greater openness. This is what matters most.

References

Alexandre, L. (1988). An inextricable mandate: Global education and multicultural studies. *Global Pages, 6*(4), 2-3, 7-8.

Anderson, W. T. (1990). *Reality isn't what it used to be.* San Francisco: HarperCollins.

Apple, M., & Beane, J. (1995). *Democratic schools.* Alexandria, VA: ASCD.

Apple, M. W. (1979). *Ideology and the curriculum.* Boston: Routledge Kegan Paul.

Bagley, W. C. (1907). *Classroom management: Its principles and techniques.* New York: Macmillan.

Baker, R. (1994, July/August). Gone with the unum. *Family Therapy Networker, 25.*

Ballenger, C. (1992). Because you like us: The language of control. *Harvard Educational Review, 62,* 199-208.

Banks, J. A. (1991). *Teaching strategies for ethnic studies.* Boston: Allyn & Bacon.

Banks, J. A. (1995). Transformative challenges to the social studies disciplines: Implications for social studies teaching and learning. *Theory and Research in Social Education, 23*(1), 2-20.

Bassey, M. O. (1993). Multicultural education: Its unexplored themes. *Western Journal of Black Studies, 17,* 202-208.

Bennett, C. I. (1995). *Comprehensive multicultural education: Theory and practice.* Boston: Allyn & Bacon.

Bennett, J. M., & Bennett, M. J. (1994). Multiculturalism and international education: Domestic and international differences. In G. Althen (Ed.), *Learning across cultures.* Washington, DC: NAFSA Association of International Educators.

Bernson, M. H., & Magnusson, E. (1989, August). *Modern Japan: An idea book for K-12 teachers.* Paper prepared as a 1983 Summer Institute Project at the East Asia Resource Center, University of Washington, Thomson Hall, DR-05, Seattle.

Biggs, J., & Moor, P. (1993). *The process of learning* (3rd ed.). Australia: Prentice Hall.

Bintz, W. P. (1995, January/February). Reflections on teaching in multicultural settings. *Social Studies,* 39-42.

Birrell, J. R. (1995). Learning how the game is played: An ethnically encapsulated beginning teacher's struggle to prepare black youth for a white world. *Teaching and Teacher Education, 11*(2), 137-147.

Bloom, B. S. (Ed.). (1956). *Taxonomy of educational objectives. Handbook 1: Cognitive domain.* New York: David McKay.

Bullough, R. V. (1994). Digging at the roots: Discipline, management, and metaphor. *Action in Teacher Education, 16*(1), 1-10.

Carger, C. L., & Ayers, W. (1995, March/April). Diverse learners in a multicultural world. *Social Studies,* 4-6.

Cornbleth, C. (1990). *Curriculum in context.* London: Falmar.

Cortés, C. (1979). Multicultural education and global education: Natural partners in the quest for a better world. In *Curricular dimensions of global education* (pp. 83-98). Philadelphia: Pennsylvania Department of Education & Research for Better Schools. (ERIC Document Reproduction Service No. ED 187 629)

Cushner, K., McClelland, A., & Safford, P. (1992). *Human diversity in education: An integrative approach.* New York: McGraw-Hill.

Davidson, A. (1994). Students' situated selves. In G. Spindler & L. Spindler (Eds.), *Pathways to cultural awareness.* Thousand Oaks, CA: Corwin Press.

DeKock, A. (1989, April). *Issues in education: Quality global/ international education: What political stance?* Report presented at the conference of The Stanley Foundation, Las Palomas de Taos, Taos, NM, & Muscatine, IA.

Delgado-Gaitan, C. (1990). *Literacy for empowerment.* Philadelphia: Falmer.

Dobyns, H. F. (1976). *Native American historical demography: A critical bibliography.* Bloomington: Indiana University Press.

Dorris, M. (1989). *The broken cord.* New York: Harper & Row.

Drum, J., & Howard, G. (1989). *Issues in education: Multicultural and global education: Seeking common ground.* Report presented at the conference of The Stanley Foundation, Las Palomas de Taos, Taos, NM, & Muscatine, IA.

Erickson, F. (1987). Transformation and school success: The politics and culture of educational achievement. *Anthropology and Education Quarterly, 18,* 335-356.

Fain, S. M. (1988). Revising the American character: Perspectives on global education and multicultural education. *Louisiana Social Studies Journal, 15*(1), 26-33.

Fine, M. (1991). *Framing dropouts.* Albany: State University of New York.

Fraser, D. (1994). Becoming familiar with classroom life. In C. McGee & D. Fraser (Eds.), *The professional practice of teaching* (pp. 15-34). Dunmore Press.

Freedman, J. F. (1995). *The obstacle course.* New York: Signet.

Frye, M. (1992). Getting it right. *Signs: Journal of Women in Culture and Society, 17,* 781-793.

Gay, G. (1988, August). Designing relevant curricula for diverse learners. *Education and Society,* 327-340.

Glazer, N. (1993, Fall). School wars: A brief history of multiculturalism in America. *The Brookings Review,* 16-19.

Gollnick, D. M., & Chinn, P. C. (1994). *Multicultural education in a pluralistic society.* New York: Macmillan.

Grant, C. A., & Sleeter, C. E. (1986). *After the school bell rings.* Philadelphia: Falmer.

Greene, M. (1994, April). *Beginnings, identities, and possibilities: The uses of social imagination.* Paper presented at the annual meeting of the American Educational Research Association, New Orleans, LA.

Hancock, L. (1996, February 19). Why do schools flunk biology? *Newsweek,* 58-59.

Harris, M. (1995). Multculturalist in training: A high school teacher's experience in developing a multicultural curriculum. *Teaching and Change, 2*(3), 275-292.

Hazelhurst, K. M. (1994). *A healing place.* Mackay, Australia: Central Queensland University Press.

Hopkins, R. (1994). *Narrative schooling.* New York: Teachers College Press.

Horowitz, D. L. (1985). *Ethnic groups in conflict.* Berkeley: University of California Press.

Hughes, R. (1993). *Culture of complaint: The fraying of America.* New York: Oxford University Press.

Jacob, E. (1995). Reflective practice and anthropology in culturally diverse classrooms. *Elementary School Journal, 95,* 451-463.

Jantz, R. K., & Weaver, P. (1992). Travel abroad as culture study. *International Journal of Social Education, 7,* 25-36.

Kemmis, S. (1986). *Curriculum theorising: Beyond reproduction theory.* Geelong, Victoria: Deakin University.

Kirchner, G. (1991). *Children's games from around the world.* Dubuque, IA: William C. Brown.

Kobus, D. K. (1989/1990). Multicultural and global education: Partners for cross-cultural understanding and citizenship education. *School of Education Journal* (California State University, Stanislaus), 7(1), 6-11.

Kobus, D. K., & Rojas, M. H. (Eds.). (1988). *From mustard seed to harvest, social studies education and teaching about women in the global community.* Report of the Wingspread Conference. Muscatine, IA: The Stanley Foundation.

Kottler, E. (1994). *Children with limited English.* Thousand Oaks, CA: Corwin Press.

Kottler, J. A. (1992). *Compassionate therapy: Working with difficult clients.* San Francisco: Jossey-Bass.

Kottler, J. A. (1994). *Beyond blame: A new way of resolving conflict in relationships.* San Francisco: Jossey-Bass.

Kottler, J. A. (1996). *The language of tears.* San Francisco: Jossey-Bass.

Kottler, J. A. (1997a). *Succeeding with difficult students.* Thousand Oaks, CA: Corwin Press.

Kottler, J. A. (1997b). *Travel that can change your life.* San Francisco: Jossey-Bass.

Kottler, J. A., Sexton, T., & Whiston, S. (1994). *Heart of healing: Relationships in therapy.* San Francisco: Jossey-Bass.

Kozol, J. (1991). *Savage inequalities: Children in America's schools.* New York: Crown.

Kozol, J. (1995). *Amazing grace: The lives of children and the conscience of a nation.* New York: Crown.

Kramer, H. (1993). Confronting the monolity. *Partisan Review, 60,* 569-684.

Ladson-Billings, G. (1994). *The dreamkeepers: Successful teachers of African American children.* San Francisco: Jossey-Bass.

Leed, E. J. (1991). *The mind of the traveler.* New York: Basic Books.

Lefrancois, G. (1991). *Psychology for teaching.* Belmont, CA: Wadsworth.

Leo, J. (1995a, February 20). The Rutgers star chamber. *U.S. News and World Report,* 22.

Leo, J. (1995b, April 10). Feel abused? Get in line. *U.S. News and World Report,* 21.

Lesko, N. (1988). *Symbolizing society: Stories, rites and structure in a Catholic high school.* New York: Falmer.

McGuiness, C., & Nisbet, J. (1991). Teaching thinking in Europe. *British Journal of Education Psychology, 61*(2), 174-186.

Mclean, C. (1995). Organising the sausage sizzle: A conversation with three young women about school. *Dulwich Centre Newsletter, 2 & 3,* 43-50.

Mead, M. (1927). The need for teaching anthropology in normal schools and teachers colleges. *School and Society, 26,* 466.

Merryfield, M. (1996a). *AACTE guidelines on multicultural education and global and international education.*

Merryfield, M. (1996b). *Teacher education in global and international education.* ERIC digest.

Merryfield, M., & Harris, J. (1992). Getting started in global education: Essential literature, essential linkages for teacher educators. *School of Education Review, 4,* 56-66.

Moll, L. C., & Diaz, S. (1993). Change as the goal of educational research. In E. Jacob & C. Jordan (Eds.), *Minority education: Anthropological perspectives.* Norwood, NJ: Ablex.

Monroe, S. S. (1992). *Margaret Mead: Anthropological perspective on educational change.* ERIC report.

More, A. J. (1993). *Adapting teaching to the learning styles of Native Indian students.* (ERIC Document Reproduction Service No. ED 366 493)

Morley, J. (1995, March/April). A PC guide to political correctness. *Family Therapy Networker*, 17-18.

Morris, J. (1943). *Traveler from Tokyo*. London: A. D. Peters.

Neki, J. S. (1976). An examination of the cultural relativism of dependence as a dynamic of social and therapeutic relationships. *British Journal of Medical Psychology, 49*, 1-10.

Nixon, H. L., & Frey, J. H. (1996). *A sociology of sport*. Belmont, CA: Wadsworth.

Perlmutter, P. (1992). *Divided we fall*. Ames: Iowa State University.

Phelan, P., Davidson, A. L., & Yu, H. C. (1993). Students' multiple worlds: Navigating the borders of family, peer, and school cultures. In P. Phelan & A. L. Davidson (Eds.), *Negotiating cultural diversity in American schools*. New York: Teachers College Press.

Powell, R. R., Zehm, S., & Garcia, J. (1996). *Field experience: Strategies for exploring diversity in schools*. Columbus, OH: Merrill.

Radosh, R. (1993). McCarthyism on the left. *Partisan Review, 60*, 677-684.

Rappaport, J. (1993). Narrative studies, personal stories, and identity transformation in the mutual help context. *Journal of Applied Behavioral Science, 29*(2), 239-256.

Riner, R. D. (1979). American Indian education: A rite that fails. *Anthropology and Education Quarterly, 10*, 236-253.

Roehrig, C. (1990). *Fun with hieroglyphs*. New York: Metropolitan Museum of Art/Viking.

Said, E. (1993). *Culture and imperialism*. New York: Knopf.

Schlesinger, A. (1992). *The disuniting of America*. New York: Norton.

Schon, D. A. (1983). *The reflective practitioner*. New York: Basic Books.

Schon, D. A. (1987). *Educating the reflective practitioner*. San Francisco: Jossey-Bass.

Shabbas, A., & Al-Qazzaz, A. (Eds.). (1989). *Arab world notebook*. Berkeley, CA: Najda: Women Concerned About the Middle East.

Slavin, R. (1990) *Cooperative learning: Theory, research, practice*. Englewood Cliffs, NJ: Prentice Hall.

Snook, I. (1992). *Teacher education: A sympathetic appraisal*. Keynote address to the conference of teacher education: An investment for New Zealand's future, Auckland, New Zealand.

Sowell, T. (1994). *Race and culture*. New York: Basic Books.

Spindler, G., & Spindler, L. (1984). *Dreamers with power: The Menomini Indians*. Prospect Heights, IL: Waveland.

Spindler, G., & Spindler, L. (1990). *The American cultural dialogue and its transmission.* London: Falmer.

Spindler, G., & Spindler, L. (1993). The process of culture and person: Cultural therapy and culturally diverse schools. In P. Phelan & A. L. Davidson (Eds.), *Negotiating cultural diversity in American schools.* New York: Teachers College Press.

Spindler, G., & Spindler, L. (1994). *Pathways to cultural awareness.* Thousand Oaks, CA: Corwin Press.

Stein, H. (1994, May). The post-sensitive man is coming. *Esquire,* pp. 56-63.

Taba, H. (1962). *Curriculum development: Theory and practice.* New York: Harcourt, Brace, & World.

Timm, J. T. (1996). *Four perspectives in multicultural education.* Belmont, CA: Wadsworth.

Trueba, H. T. (1993). Cultural diversity and conflict: The role of educational anthropology in healing multicultural America. In P. Phelan & A. L. Davidson (Eds.), *Negotiating cultural diversity in American schools.* New York: Teachers College Press.

Turner, V. W. (1966). *The ritual process: Structure and anti-structure.* Chicago: Aldine.

Turner, V. W. (1992). *Blazing the trail.* Tucson: University of Arizona Press.

Tye, K. A. (Ed.). (1990). *Global education: School-based strategies.* Orange, CA: Interdependence.

Von Glasersfeld, E. (1990). An exposition of constructivism: Why some like it radical. *Journal for Research in Mathematics Education* (Monograph No. 4).

Weaver, G. R. (1995). Communication and conflict in the multicultural classroom. *Adult Learning, 6*(5), 23-24.

Wente, M. (1995, March 31). Female republicans back off Newt. *Times Columnist,* p. C2.

White, M. (1995). Schools as communities of acknowledgement: A conversation with Michael White. *Dulwich Centre Newsletter, 2 & 3,* 51-66.

White, M., & Epston, D. (1989). *Literate means to therapeutic ends.* Adelaide, Australia: Dulwich Centre.

Will, G. (1996, February 19). Intellectual segregation. *Newsweek,* 78.

Wilson, A. (1993). Conservation partners: Helping students gain a global perspective through cross-cultural experiences. *Theory Into Practice, 32*(1), 21-26.

Wilson, A. (1996). Connections between multicultural education and global education. In R. Powell (Ed.), *Multicultural and global education: Together in multiculturalism and reform.* Lexington: University of Kentucky, Institute of Educational Reform.

Wilson, P. (1991). Trauma of Sioux Indian high school students. *Anthropology and Education Quarterly, 22,* 367-383.

Wittrock, M. C. (1977). Learning as a generative process. In M. C. Wittrock (Ed.), *Learning and instruction.* Berkeley, CA: McCutcheon.

Wright, R. (1994). *The moral animal.* New York: Pantheon.

Zehm, S., & Kottler, J. A. (1993). *On being a teacher: The human dimension.* Thousand Oaks, CA: Corwin Press.